S0-BAT-048

Easy Nitrox Diving
Nitrox Diving Using Dive Computers

by
Steven M. Barsky

Published by
Scuba Diving International
Topsham, Maine

Easy Nitrox Diving
Nitrox Diving Using Dive Computers
by Steven M. Barsky

Scuba Diving International
18 Elm Street
Topsham, ME 04086
Tel: 207-729-4201
FAX: 207-729-4453

Find us on the World Wide Web at http://www.tdisdi.com/

© 2001 International Training, Inc.

Photography
Principal photography by Bret Gilliam. ©Bret Gilliam. All rights reserved.
Additional photography by Steven M. Barsky and Wayne Hasson.

Primary photo models: Lynn Hendrickson, Cathryn Castle, Lina Hitchcock, Gretchen Gilliam, Tom Burgener, George Stuart, Tanya Brungard, Kristine Barsky, Andrew Dawson, and Scott Lockwood.

Illustrations:
© Steven M. Barsky. All rights reserved.

Notice of Rights:
All rights reserved. No part of this book may be reproduced or transmitted in any form by any means, electronic, mechanical, photocopying, recording, or otherwise without the prior written permission of the publisher. For information on getting permission for reprints and excerpts, contact Scuba Diving International.

Printed by Ojai Printing, Ojai, CA

ISBN Number:1-931451-00-1

Library of Congress Control Number: 2001089000

Other Titles Available from Scuba Diving International

Training Manual for Scuba Diving: Dive Training for the 21st Century
Easy Nitrox Diving
Deeper Diving with Dive Computers
Wreck Diving and Boat Diving Techniques
Rescue Diving Manual: A Guide to Rescue Techniques, Stress, Injury, and
        Accident Management
Dry Suit Diving
Solo Diving Techniques: A Manual for Independent Diving Skills
Visual Inspection Procedures: A Manual for Cylinder Safety
CPROX: Guidelines for Essential CPR and Oxygen Administration
CPR-FIRST: A Concise Manual for Emergency First Aid and CPR

Other Titles Available from Technical Diving International

Nitrox Diver Manual
Advanced Nitrox Diver Manual
Decompression Procedures
Semi-Closed Circuit Rebreather Manual: Draeger Units
Trimix Diving Manual
Extended Range Diver Manual
Cave and cavern Diving Manual
Advanced Wreck Diving
Deep Diving: An Advanced Guide to Physiology, Procedures, and Systems
Nitrox Blending Manual: Guide to Preparation of Oxygen Enriched Air
Advanced Gas Blending Manual: Nitrox, Trimix, and Custom Mixes

WARNING!

Nitrox diving is an activity in which divers use breathing gases that contain elevated levels of oxygen, beyond the 21% found in normal air. There are risks in nitrox diving that go beyond the usual risks associated with recreational scuba diving.

Although this book was written specifically for an instructional course devoted to using nitrox mixtures containing up to and including 40% oxygen, it is understood that people make mistakes and misunderstand each other. For this reason, anyone who uses nitrox must be aware of the special risks to which one is exposed when using breathing mixtures with elevated levels of oxygen.

Breathing gas mixtures that contain more than 40% oxygen are subject to fires and explosions if improperly handled. Although this course material is designed to train divers who will use mixtures containing up to and including 40% oxygen, as a nitrox diver, you may be exposed to these risks by having your cylinders filled at a nitrox facility or by being in the vicinity of other divers who are using mixtures that contain greater than 40% oxygen.

Any time a diver uses nitrox underwater there are also additional risks including temporary visual and hearing disturbances, irritability, nausea, dizziness, and convulsions. Visual and hearing disturbances and irritability can lead a person to make incorrect choices in an emergency situation. Nausea and dizziness can lead to vomiting underwater, which can lead to drowning and death. Convulsions underwater almost always lead to drowning and death. Although these risks are small when using nitrox containing up to and including 40% oxygen (EAN 40), every diver must be aware of and know how to avoid these risks. This book is designed to provide information to help the diver avoid these problems.

Table of Contents

Table of Contents

Foreword

Bret Gilliam, CEO Scuba Diving Intnl.

I started diving nitrox mixes as a Navy diver back in 1971. Back then we called the new gas "oxy-air". Many years later it was formalized in the NOAA diving program for scientists working in the oceans.

Our sister company, Technical Diving International or TDI, pioneered nitrox training programs and has certified more nitrox divers and instructors than any other agency. With a bit of hindsight, it's interesting to note that nitrox was originally considered to be "technical" in nature and was removed from traditional sport training curricula.

We always thought that such a distinction was undeserved and that the technology of nitrox was actually a very simple academic subject to teach. In fact, one diving leader responded to critics who suggested that nitrox was "too complicated for the regular diving public" by saying, "nitrox is as simple as: breathe in, breathe out, repeat as necessary, don't dive below 130 feet."

Essentially he was correct and the initial controversy over nitrox in the early 1990's gave way to universal acceptance. Now it's rare indeed to visit a tropical dive resort or liveaboard vessel that does not offer nitrox.

But the biggest breakthrough for divers was the launch of modern dive computers that could be programmed for varying nitrox mixes (and air). Now divers had the equivalent of radios that played all the stations, not just one. Nitrox popularity soared.

As you'll learn in this book, nitrox allows divers to extend no-decompression bottom times and reduce surface intervals between dives. This all adds up to an enhanced diving experience. Not only is it more convenient to plan nitrox dives with computers, it's safer.

Nitrox has a variety of other applications in diving interests you may choose to pursue later including planned decompression diving and rebreather apparatus. Rebreathers can eliminate bubble exhausts and allow close encounters with wary marine life such as sharks and whales.

This text is designed to give you the most "user friendly" guide to nitrox diving possible. It will introduce you to a better way to dive that will make you more efficient and give you more time underwater to enjoy our fascinating sport.

This is the first book ever published that is devoted to teaching nitrox exclusively with dive computers. Steve Barsky has done an excellent job of providing you a text that covers all the bases... but won't wear you out with non-essential information.

It's a great technology. Use it wisely to make your diving experience better and safer.

Bret Gilliam
President and CEO
SCUBA DIVING INTERNATIONAL

Acknowledgements

For many years, nitrox diving has been taught in the traditional fashion, where students learn the formulas for calculating equivalent air depths, maximum operating depths, partial pressures, and other numbers which they promptly forget how to use. In the real world, the greatest majority of divers buy nitrox dive computers and go on about their diving without ever performing a mathematical calculation.

When Bret Gilliam first suggested the idea for this book, we started with the premise of only teaching EAN 32, i.e., nitrox containing 32% oxygen. However, as the work on the book progressed, it quickly became apparent that we could teach divers how to use nitrox mixtures up to and including EAN 40 using this text. While some people in the diving industry may be shocked or even outraged by this text, this is the way that divers use nitrox in the real world.

Thanks to Bret, you are holding the most up-to-date approach for teaching nitrox diving available. I especially appreciate the opportunity he provided me in asking me to write this text.

Numerous other people and companies provided the assistance we needed to bring this project to completion. I am deeply indebted to the following:

- Wayne Hasson - Aggressor Fleet
- Harry Averill with Dive-Rite
- Brian Carney at TDI/SDI Headquarters
- Jim Clymer at AquaLung/Seaquest
- Lynn Hendrickson at TDI/SDI
- Joel Silverstein with Abyssmal Diving Products
- Jamie Spicer at Scubapro/Uwatec
- John Wall at The Dive Shop, Fairfax, Virginia
- Ron Grzelka at Atlanta Swim and Scuba Academy
- Rob Arnold at Atlanta Swim and Scuba Academy
- Cliff Simoneau

Finally, I would like to thank my wife, Kristine Barsky, who is my equal partner in all of my projects. Without her support and assistance, nothing I do would ever be as complete as I envision it.

Steven M. Barsky
Santa Barbara, CA

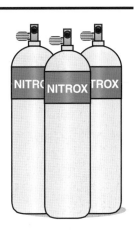

Chapter 1
Nitrox Diving is Simple!

As divers, it seems that we can never spend enough time underwater. Almost every dive, but especially the deeper ones, is too short. When the water is warm and clear, normal surface intervals often seem way too long.

There is a way to extend your dives, dramatically, and to shorten your surface intervals. To do this, we use a breathing gas called "nitrox."

You've probably heard of nitrox, although you may have heard it called by a variety of names, including enriched air, oxygen enriched air, EAN, EANx, NOAA Nitrox I or II, and SafeAir. Some people jokingly refer to nitrox as the "fat and over 40 gas," for reasons you'll learn shortly, although nitrox offers benefits to all divers. What's important to know is that all of these terms refer to the same thing, i.e., nitrox.

The compressed air that we use for scuba diving is a mixture of primarily two gases, oxygen and nitrogen. The normal percentage of each gas in the mixture is about 79% nitrogen and 21% oxygen. Nitrox is also a mixture of nitrogen and oxygen, but it has more oxygen than normal air.

The percentage of oxygen in nitrox can be varied according to your individual needs. It is specially mixed at the dive store by a trained person known as a "nitrox blender" when your tank is filled. You specify exactly how much oxygen you want in the "mix" and the blender does the rest.

Nitrogen and oxygen can be mixed in any ratio, but the most commonly used mixtures are as follows:

- 68% nitrogen, 32% oxygen
- 64% nitrogen, 36% oxygen
- 60% nitrogen, 40% oxygen
- 50% nitrogen, 50% oxygen
- 40% nitrogen, 60% oxygen

There are two big advantages to using nitrox. First, by increasing the amount of oxygen in your breathing gas, you can increase your maximum

© Aqua Lung

You will learn to use your nitrox comput-er to avoid decompression and monitor your oxygen exposure.

allowable bottom time. This happens because there is less nitrogen in the mix to be absorbed by your body. The more oxygen there is in the mixture, the longer you extend your bottom time, within certain limits. Secondly, since you are absorbing less nitrogen on a given dive, your surface intervals can usually be shortened. To dive nitrox effectively, we use special nitrox dive computers.

Another way that divers use nitrox is to dive with nitrox, but use a dive computer designed for air diving and follow the air diving times and surface intervals calculated by their computer. Older divers who are out of shape, or divers who have suffered from decompression sickness, feel that by using nitrox conservatively in this way, they improve their chances of avoiding decompression sickness. While many divers and medical experts believe that this concept is probably correct, at the time of this publication, there have been no scientific tests to prove this theory.

Some divers report that by using nitrox they suffer from less fatigue after diving. Others believe that by using nitrox they will be less susceptible to nitrogen narcosis at depth.

Once your tank is filled with nitrox you'll find that it does not make you feel any differently underwater than breathing ordinary compressed air. In most respects, you will be able to dive with nitrox without making any marked changes in your diving.

When you dive with nitrox, you must monitor your exposure to increased levels of oxygen, just as you monitor your bottom time and depth to avoid decompression. When your dive computer is properly set for the oxygen mix-ture you are using, it will monitor your oxygen exposure and decompression status automatically. Each nitrox mixture has a maximum operating depth (MOD) beyond which it must not be used. You'll learn more about this in the next chapter.

For any given nitrox mixture, you have a time limitation for oxygen exposure at its maximum operating depth of 45 minutes for any single dive. Over the course of a 24-hour period, you have a cumulative time limit for oxygen exposure at the maximum operating depth of two and a half hours in any 24-hour period. With most dive computers, you will reach your no-decompression limits before you ever experience a limitation due to your oxygen exposure.

This exposure to higher levels of oxygen carries a certain level of risk, similar to the level of risk of decompression sickness. This will be explained in further detail in Chapter 3, which defines the risks of nitrox diving. From a practical standpoint, most divers will not have a problem with oxygen exposures if they observe normal sport diving limits, avoid decompression or borderline no-decompression situations, and observe reasonable surface intervals.

Using Nitrox

In this course you will learn to dive with nitrox mixtures with various combinations of nitrogen and oxygen, up to a maximum of 60% nitrogen, 40% oxygen. This mixture is more properly referred to as EAN 40 (Enriched air nitrox 40). These mixtures – EAN 32, EAN 36, and EAN 40 are the simplest and most versatile nitrox mixtures to use, and they can be used without learning any mathematical formulas.

Nitrox has become very popular with divers.

During this course, you will learn how to perform the following:

• Set your dive computer for the proper percentage of oxygen in your mixture.
• Monitor your oxygen exposure using your dive computer while diving.
• Use your computer for planning your initial and repetitive dives (assuming your computer has both of these capabilities).
• Use a table or your dive computer to determine the maximum depth for your nitrox mix.

Gas mixtures containing 40% oxygen or less are considered appropriate for "basic" nitrox divers. Gas mixtures containing more than 40% oxygen are sometimes called "advanced nitrox" or "technical nitrox."

Are you ready to start enjoying longer dives with shorter surface intervals? Let's get started with easy nitrox diving!

How to Use this Book

This book will be a reference for you to use during this course. It is essential for you to read and understand all of the information in this book. If any of the material in this book is unclear to you, please discuss the concepts with your instructor so that you understand all of the information. It is essential for you to understand how to use nitrox effectively, as well as the risks in using nitrox, before you dive with nitrox in open water.

Don't hesitate to take this book with you on your openwater diving trips to refresh your understanding of the concepts of nitrox diving between dives. Just be careful, because divers who don't understand nitrox will probably want to borrow your book and may not want to give it back to you!

Scuba I.Q. Review

At the end of each chapter of this book we will present a series of review questions that your SDI diving instructor will discuss with you. You must understand the concept behind each aspect of using nitrox in order to dive with nitrox correctly.

1) List two other commonly used terms to describe nitrox.

2) State the normal percentages of oxygen and nitrogen in air.

3) Define the term "nitrox."

4) What is the name for a person who fills scuba tanks with nitrox?

5) List two common nitrox mixtures used by divers.

6) State the two advantages of using nitrox.

7) Disregarding decompression, what is the maximum total amount of bottom time that you can use a nitrox mixture at its maximum operating depth in any 24-hour period?

Chapter 2
How Nitrox Works to Give You More Bottom Time

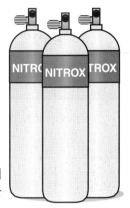

To use nitrox effectively, you need to understand the concepts behind how it works. In this chapter we'll review the concepts behind no-decompression diving, decompression sickness, and gas mixtures other than air. When you're finished reading this chapter you should understand how nitrox works to give you longer bottom times and shorter surface intervals.

Understanding Nitrogen and Decompression

As a diver, you know that air contains a mixture of approximately 79% nitrogen and 21% oxygen. At the surface, the nitrogen inside your body is in balance with the air outside your body.

When you dive, as the pressure increases on your body, your regulator supplies air at a pressure exactly equal to the surrounding pressure. Since the concentration of nitrogen in the air you are breathing is greater than the amount of nitrogen in your body's tissues, your body absorbs more nitrogen at depth. The deeper you dive and the longer you stay underwater, the more nitrogen you will absorb through your lungs into your blood stream. From your blood stream, the nitrogen is carried throughout your body.

You wear a dive computer underwater to calculate the amount of nitrogen absorbed by your body, and indicate to you when it is time to ascend. The dive computer provides a theoretical model of what is happening inside your body, but it does not mirror the exact physiological mechanisms inside your body. Someday we may have dive computers implanted inside our bodies, but at the present time they don't exist!

As you return to the surface, and the pressure decreases, this extra nitrogen that you absorbed at depth must be released from your body. If your dive was not too deep or too long, you can make a normal ascent to the surface. However, if your dive lasted for a long time, or you made a deep dive, your dive computer will indicate that you must stop at a particular depth to allow

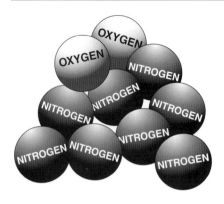

Air is a mixture of 21% oxygen and 79% nitrogen.

the excess nitrogen in your body time to escape without causing problems. Your computer may require you to make one stop, or a series of stops, commonly known as "decompression stops." During these decompression stops, the excess nitrogen in your body is carried back to the lungs where you exhale it each time you breathe. Smart divers always make a precautionary decompression stop, usually referred to as a "safety stop," for 3-5 minutes at a depth of 10-15 feet at the end of every dive.

You can also incur a decompression obligation by making repetitive dives over a period of time. While no one dive by itself may exceed the no-decompression limit for a particular depth, nitrogen can accumulate in your body over a series of dives, leading to a decompression obligation for a dive which, by itself, would normally be considered a no-decompression dive.

Decompression diving is not recommended without specific training.

Sport divers should avoid decompression diving.

©2000 Steven M. Barsky. All rights reserved.

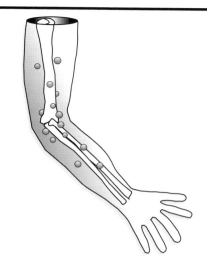

Decompression sickness occurs when there is excess nitrogen in your body.

If you have a problem during a decompression dive that prevents you from making your required stops, you are at a greater risk of suffering from decompression sickness.

Sport divers should avoid decompression diving by using their dive computers to plan their dives, and carefully monitoring their computers during their dives. However, even if you follow your dive computer's recommendations for dive times and ascent rates and dive within the no-decompression limits, there is always a slight but real risk that you could suffer from decompression sickness (DCS). The same risks exist when you use dive tables.

Decompression sickness usually occurs when you have an excess amount of nitrogen in your body and you ascend too quickly. The most common symptoms include, but are not limited to, pain in the joints, numbness, paralysis, loss of balance, muscle weakness, and impaired thinking. First aid for decompression sickness includes having the diver lie down and providing pure oxygen. Proper treatment requires recompression in a hyperbaric chamber.

Recompression treatment is expensive and time consuming. The procedure involves placing the diver inside a recompression (hyperbaric) chamber and pressurizing the chamber, usually to a depth of 60 feet. The diver is then brought back to the surface very slowly, during which time there are extended periods where he breathes pure oxygen. Even with prompt, rapid treatment, not all divers who suffer from decompression sickness fully recover. All nitrox divers should observe prudent dive planning and perform safety stops as a precaution to help prevent decompression sickness.

Using Nitrox to Extend Bottom Time & Avoid Decompression

Many years ago, scientists realized that they could extend the amount of time a diver could work underwater by increasing the amount of oxygen and decreasing the amount of nitrogen in his breathing mixture. Through calculation and experimentation they came up with a series of dive tables used to determine the no-decompression limits for different mixtures of oxygen and nitrogen. This was done in the years before anyone had heard of a dive computer.

On the surface, you can breathe gas mixtures containing as little as 16% oxygen and still maintain consciousness. Topside you can also breathe 100% pure oxygen (without any nitrogen), as we already mentioned, which is used in the treatment of decompression sickness.

Underwater, sport, technical, and commercial divers may use different gas mixtures other than normal air. Sport divers use mixtures of nitrox with up to 40% oxygen in the mix. Technical divers, who dive outside of the sport diving limits, may use multiple gas mixtures on a single dive, by carrying multiple cylinders, or using special diving gear known as "rebreathers." On deeper dives they may use gas mixtures with less than 16% oxygen for the deep part of their dives and up to 100% oxygen during the decompression phase of their dives.

Commercial divers, who dive to depths in excess of 1000 feet of sea

©OMS. All rights reserved.

Divers use different gas mixtures depending on the type of dive they are doing.

water, use gas mixtures combining helium and oxygen. Helium is used for very deep dives because it has little narcotic effect when compared to nitrogen. The gas mixture for an extended dive to 400 feet by a commercial diver might typically be 96% helium and only 4% oxygen!

During World War II, military divers found that they could dive with 100% oxygen, but only use this mixture down to a depth of about 20 feet. Below that depth, something about the oxygen caused divers to go into convulsions without warning. This was almost always fatal. Today, we have a better, but still incomplete understanding of why oxygen rich breathing mixtures pose problems for divers when used at depth.

We've also discovered that divers who use ordinary compressed air to depths in excess of 218 feet of sea water can suffer the same type of convulsions experienced by divers who use pure oxygen to depths in excess of 20 feet. It has been shown mathematically that breathing the oxygen in compressed air at a depth of 218 feet of sea water is roughly the equivalent of breathing pure oxygen at a depth greater than 20 feet of sea water.

This information is presented so that you can appreciate the complexities that technical divers must face. For sport diving, we use a limited number of standard mixtures of nitrogen and oxygen that work within the range of sport diving depths.

With the proper training and equipment, there are many breathing mixtures that can be used in diving. For the sport diver, nitrox represents the most convenient and economical. As you continue your diver training you may want to learn how to use other breathing mixtures, but nitrox will always be the easiest alternative breathing gas to use for diving.

Equivalent Air Depth

Another concept that you will hear frequently in relation to nitrox is what is known as the "equivalent air depth." Just as we stated above that using pure oxygen at 20 feet of seawater is like using compressed air at 218 feet, we can make similar computations for any depth we choose.

The equivalent air depth is used to compare nitrogen levels for calculating bottom time. In computing the equivalent air depth, what we are really saying is that a dive to a certain number of feet of seawater on nitrox is equivalent to a dive to a depth of a lesser number of feet on air.

In the early days of nitrox diving, when divers used decompression tables, they had to compute the equivalent air depth for every dive they made. With the dive computers that we use today, this is no longer necessary. The following tables show the equivalent air depths for nitrox mixtures from EAN 32 through EAN40.

Equvalent Air Depths in Feet			
Actual Depth	EAN 32	EAN 36	EAN 40
40	30	26	22
50	38	34	30
60	47	42	38
70	56	50	45
80	64	59	53
90	73	67	60
100	81	75	68
110	90	83	N/A
120	99	91	N/A
130	107	N/A	N/A

To understand the equivalent air depth table, look at the column for EAN 32 at a depth of 70 feet. If you are breathing EAN 32 at 70 feet of sea water (FSW), the decreased amount of nitrogen in the mix will be absorbed by your body as if you were only diving at 56 FSW. With EAN 36 at 70 feet of sea water, it is as though you were diving at 50 FSW. Diving with EAN 40 to 70 FSW, your body absorbs nitrogen as though you were at 45 FSW. Clearly, the more oxygen there is in the gas mixture you are breathing, the longer you can stay at any given depth without incurring a decompression obligation. A more detailed Equivalent Air Depth table can be found in the back of the book.

What is the Optimum Nitrox Mixture for Sport Diving?

There is an optimum nitrox mixture for any depth to which sport divers normally dive, down to 132 feet of sea water. That mixture is 68% nitrogen and 32% oxygen (EAN 32). The actual maximum operating depth for EAN 32 is 132 feet of seawater (FSW), but typically this is "rounded up" to 130 FSW since it matches what has been the traditional recommended depth limit for sport diving training.

The reason EAN 32 is considered the optimum nitrox mixture is because it is the most oxygen rich mixture that you can use down to the traditional recommended sport diving depth limit of 130 FSW. Gas mixtures containing

© S. Barsky. All rights reserved.

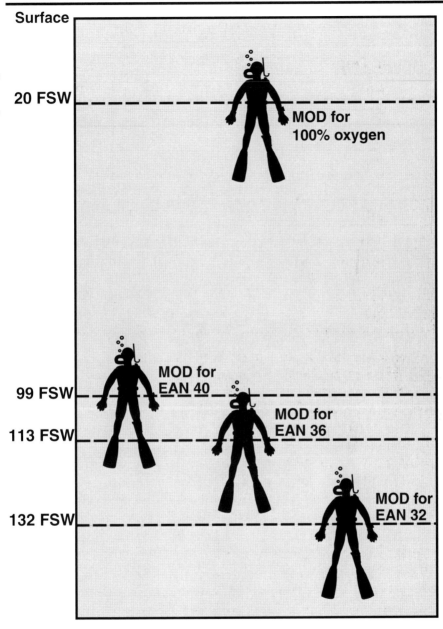

Each nitrox mixture has its own Maximum Operating Depth (MOD) which must not be exceeded. Most nitrox texts will round up the numbers for the MODs to the closest 10 foot increment. Since modern dive computers allow you to monitor your depth to the foot, SDI/TDI considers it acceptable to use the exact depths that are the established limits for each mixture.

a higher percentage of oxygen are not safe at this depth.

The higher the percentage of oxygen used in the mixture, the shallower the "Maximum Operating Depth" or "M.O.D." is for a particular mixture. As mentioned previously, a nitrox diver can select a particular mixture for his planned depth. The key word here is "planned," because the more oxygen in the mix, the more restricted the maximum operating depth. When you decide to dive with nitrox, you must plan your dive starting at the dive store when you have your tank filled.

For example, if you dive with a mixture of 40% nitrogen and 60% oxygen, EAN 60, your maximum operating depth must not exceed 55 feet of sea water. Since you need to choose your mixture when you have your tank filled at the dive store, selecting EAN 60 is very restrictive unless you know for a fact you will not be exceeding this depth on your dives.

The maximum operating depth for EAN 36 is 113 FSW and the maximum operating depth for EAN 40 is 99 FSW. When figuring oxygen determined depth limits, it has been common practice to "round up" to the next shallower ten foot increment. For example, 113 FSW becomes 110 FSW and

The blender will not always be able to fill your cylinder to the exact percentage of oxygen that you specify.

55 FSW becomes 50 FSW and so on. Note that as the percentage of oxygen in the mixture increases, the maximum operating depth decreases (becomes shallower). When your tank is filled with nitrox, the blender will not always be able to fill your tank with the exact percentage of oxygen that you specify, due to variations in gas temperature, rounding of numbers, and other factors. You must know the exact percentage of oxygen in your tank to adjust your dive computer properly for the dive.

If you look at the Equivalent Air Depth Table you will note that the bottom row of the table "stair-steps" upwards, from left to right. The numbers in the bottom row for each gas mixture are the maximum operating depths for each particular nitrox mix.

EAN 32 will provide you with a good combination of extended bottom time and unrestricted depth within the sport diving range. In addition, using EAN 32 poses less risk in terms of exposure to oxygen than other "richer" mixtures. You'll learn more about the risks in using nitrox in the next chapter.

Concept of Partial Pressure

There is one more concept that we must understand to use nitrox properly. This is the concept of "partial pressure." There are mathematical formulas for computing partial pressure that you must know if you are using a wide variety of nitrox mixtures that contain more than 40% oxygen.

In any mixture of two or more gases, such as nitrogen and oxygen, each gas occupies a certain part of the mixture and exerts a certain part of the total pressure exerted by that gas. This portion of the pressure is called, logically enough, its "partial pressure."

The partial pressure of oxygen can be expressed in pounds per square inch or in "atmospheres." One atmosphere is equal to the pressure at sea level, or the weight of all of the air above you that presses down on your body. Every 33 feet we descend in the ocean is equal to an additional atmosphere of pressure. At a depth of 33 feet in the ocean we are exposed to two atmospheres of pressure, i.e., the total of the weight of the atmosphere plus the weight of 33 feet of sea water equals two atmospheres.

Our bodies can tolerate pure oxygen at a depth of 20 feet of sea water, which is equal to 1.6 atmospheres. For sport diving purposes, we can use EAN 32 properly down to 132 feet of sea water where the pressure of the oxygen in the mixture is equal to 1.6 atmospheres. Breathing pure oxygen at a depth of 20 feet of sea water is the equivalent of breathing EAN 32 at 132 feet of sea water.

You will frequently see the partial pressure of oxygen referred to as "ppO_2" or more correctly, as "PO_2." The "pp" or "P" is an abbreviation for "partial pressure" and "O_2" is the chemical symbol for oxygen. There is nothing magical about this term, and for our purposes all you need to know is that your maximum PO_2 must never exceed 1.6. You need to know this information to set and use your nitrox dive computer properly.

Scuba I.Q. Review

Now that you know a bit about gas mixtures other than normal air, discuss these topics with your instructor. You should be able to answer any of the following questions.

1) State the cause of decompression sickness.

2) Explain how a dive computer is used to help avoid decompression sickness.

3) Define the term, "decompression stop."

4) Explain three reasons why sport divers should avoid decompression diving.

5) List three symptoms of decompression sickness.

6) State the recommended first aid for decompression sickness.

7) State the proper treatment of decompression sickness.

8) State the minimum amount of oxygen required to maintain consciousness on the surface.

9) State the maximum percentage of oxygen that sport divers use in a nitrox mixture.

10) State the maximum recommended depth for using 100% oxygen.

11) Define the term "M.O.D." and explain its use in nitrox diving.

12) Define the term "EAN 32."

13) State the M.O.D. for EAN 32.

14) List two reasons why EAN 32 is a good choice for nitrox diving.

15) State the maximum partial pressure of oxygen we use in nitrox diving.

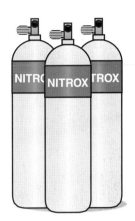

Chapter 3
Risks In Nitrox Diving

Every type of diving involves some risk because diving is an adventure sport. However, we can minimize the risks through proper instruction, using and maintaining quality diving equipment, staying in good physical condition, and participating in diving on a regular basis.

You are engaged in a nitrox diving course that will teach you the proper techniques for using nitrox mixtures up to and including EAN 40. In this course you will also learn how to select the proper equipment for this type of diving, and how to recognize and easily avoid the risks in using nitrox.

The risks presented here are not intended to scare you. At Scuba Diving International we believe that you should have a full understanding of all the potential risks in diving. However, these risks can be avoided with proper training, which is what this course is all about. In this chapter you'll learn about these risks, but more importantly, how to easily avoid them.

Oxygen Toxicity

Oxygen toxicity (also referred to as "oxygen poisoning") is a physiological reaction of your body that occurs when you are exposed to breathing mixtures containing high percentages of oxygen, or mixtures containing lower percentages of oxygen for extended periods. Exactly how and why the human body responds in this way is not fully understood, but the effect is like "short circuiting" your nervous system.

When a diver experiences an oxygen "hit," the results can occur without warning and the consequences can frequently be fatal. The effects of oxygen poisoning are easily remembered by the acronym, "CONVENTID." Each one of the letters in this word stands for a specific effect.

CON – stands for convulsions, the most dangerous and potentially fatal risk in using nitrox. The convulsions that occur during oxygen poisoning are similar to an epileptic seizure and may occur without warning. When a convulsion occurs underwater, drowning and death frequently occur. The remaining symptoms may or may not occur prior to a convulsion.

©Steven M. Barsky. All rights reserved.

Convulsions are a real risk for nitrox divers who use this gas mixture carelessly.

V – The "V" in CONVENTID stands for visual disturbances, which may take the form of "tunnel vision" or the perception of bright flashes of light when nothing is there.

E – The "E" stands for ringing in the ears and other auditory hallucinations.

N – The second "N" stands for nausea. Vomiting underwater is distinctly unpleasant and dangerous.

T – The "T" represents twitching of the muscles, particularly the cheek, nose or eyelids.

I – The "I" indicates irritability or apprehension.

D – The "D" stands for dizziness.

If your diving partner has a convulsion you want to get them to the surface immediately. If you or your partner experience any of the other symptoms of oxygen poisoning, you should immediately ascend to a shallower depth and make a normal ascent to the surface. These other symptoms indi-

©Steven M. Barsky. All rights reserved.

Other effects of oxygen toxicity include visual disturbances, auditory hallucinations, nausea, muscle twitching, irritability, and dizziness.

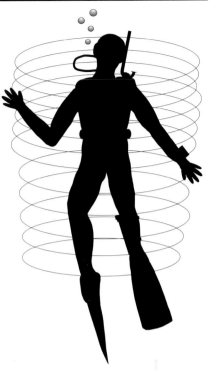

cate oxygen poisoning is happening and may occur before a convulsion as a warning.

Fortunately, the effects of oxygen toxicity usually only occur when you have violated the maximum depth limit (MOD) for the mixture you are using. Once you ascend to a shallower depth or exit the water, the symptoms disappear and there appears to be no permanent damage.

To the best of our knowledge, no one who has used EAN 32 and followed the proper procedures for diving with this gas has ever experienced these symptoms. However, if you violate the maximum operating depth of 132 feet these effects can occur without warning. Always pay strict attention to ensure you are not exceeding the maximum operating depth of your mix.

Similar to the way in which exposure to increased nitrogen at depth causes your body to absorb more nitrogen, exposures to higher levels of oxygen at depth causes your body to become more sensitive to increased levels of oxygen during subsequent dives. Each dive you make with nitrox during any given 24-hour period increases your oxygen exposure.

Additional Precautions While Diving

There are other factors that can increase the possibility of an "attack" of oxygen poisoning. These factors include the following:

- If you overheat during a dive.
- If you are an insulin dependent diabetic.
- If you suffer from a deficiency of Vitamin E.
- If you have an overactive thyroid (hyperthyroid) gland.
- Diving without proper thermal protection in cold water.
- Other drugs that may speed the onset of oxygen toxicity include

adrenocortical hormones, dextroamphetamine, epinephrine, norepi-nephrine, and paraquat.
- If you are making a dive where you are working or swimming hard underwater.
- If you have scar tissue in your lungs you may be more susceptible to oxygen poisoning.

If you suffer from any of the medical problems listed above, or are taking any of the drugs listed above, you must discuss this with your instructor and you will need medical clearance to dive nitrox. To reduce your risk when using nitrox, if any of the above conditions apply to you, you must avoid diving nitrox to its maximum operating depth. For example, to be more conservative in using EAN 32, you would not use this gas at its maximum operating depth and restrict your diving to depths of 120 FSW or shallower to lessen the PO_2.

You may also hear people discuss the possibility of lung irritation when using nitrox for extended periods. This is not a problem in normal recreational diving.

Precautions to Avoid Oxygen Toxicity

Fortunately, avoiding these negative effects of oxygen is easy when using EAN mixtures. Just follow these precautions and you should never have a problem using nitrox:

Diving without proper thermal protection in cold water can speed the onset of oxygen toxicity. In cold water, a dry suit is recommended. To take advantage of the long bottom times provided by nitrox, you must have sufficient thermal protection.

Photo by S. Barsky. Courtesy Diving Unlimited International.

Avoid making extended dives that take you right up to the maximum operating depth for the mixture you are using!

- Avoid overheating.
- Avoid extended dives to the Maximum Operating Depth for the mixture you are using.
- Wear adequate thermal protection while diving in cold water.
- Never dive with nitrox deeper than the MOD for the mix you are using.
- Avoid heavy exercise while diving with nitrox.
- Get medical clearance for diving if you are an insulin dependent diabetic. If cleared to dive, restrict your diving to shallower depths.
- Get medical clearance for diving if you are taking any of the other drugs listed in this chapter and still want to use nitrox. If cleared to dive, restrict your diving to shallower depths.

If you work hard underwater, like this diver using a hammer, or even swimming against a current, these activities can hasten the onset of oxygen toxicity.

Remember that diving to 132 feet of sea water on EAN 32 exposes you to the maximum allowable partial pressure of oxygen, or a PO$_2$ of 1.6. Other mixtures have shallower depth limits. If you want to be more conservative, limit your diving to shallower depths.

Nitrox Repetitive Dive Limitations

Just as you have no-decompression limits in diving due to nitrogen adsorption in our bodies, we have additional limits imposed on us when we use nitrox for diving. If you use nitrogen mixtures that contain high percentages of oxygen, such as EAN 40, or above, these limits can become quite restrictive. However, using EAN 32 rarely imposes any additional limits on our diving. You just need to be aware of them and monitor for them.

There are various terms that are used to denote your exposure to higher levels of oxygen while diving with nitrox. You may hear people talk about CNS (Central Nervous System) oxygen limits, OTUs (Oxygen Tolerance Units), OLF (Oxygen Limit Fraction), OTLs (Oxygen Time Limits), or use other terminology. At Scuba Diving International we prefer to use the term Oxygen Time Limit when we are referring to the maximum exposure you can have to enriched oxygen mixtures underwater. However, your nitrox dive computer may use slightly different terminology. It is important for you to understand how your computer measures oxygen exposure and provides warnings for this aspect of your dives.

Nitrox dive computers are designed to compute oxygen exposures, no-decompression limits, and repetitive dive information for the specific gas mixture you are using. For your computer to work properly, it must be set for the mixture you are using **before** you enter the water. You will learn more about this in the chapters on equipment selection, dive planning, and making nitrox dives. If you are using an air diving computer, rather than a nitrox computer, you will be limited by the no-decompression limits of your computer to such an extent that oxygen exposure will not be a problem.

Almost all modern dive computers provide alarms that will warn you when you are reaching the limits of oxygen exposure for the time, depth, and mixture you are using. Some will also be set to activate an alarm when you reach the maximum PO$_2$ for the mixture in your tank. These alarms may be both visual and audible. Some computers also compare decompression time, oxygen exposure, and gas consumption and provide warnings about which of these factors will most immediately affect your dive.

As a point of reference, the table on this page provides a comparison of time and depth limits for a single dive (not a repetitive dive) using EAN 32, EAN 36, and EAN 40 compared to ordinary air. These numbers are based on dive tables and do **not** represent the times allowed by dive computers.

Comparison of Single Dive Times Using Nitrox and Compressed Air				
Depth in Feet	Air	EAN 32	EAN 36	EAN 40
40	200	400	400	400
50	100	200	200	300
60	60	100	100	200
70	50	60	60	100
80	40	50	60	60
90	30	40	50	60
100	25	30	40	45* @99'
110	20	25	40	N/A
120	15	25	N/A	N/A
130	10	20	N/A	N/A

* **Actual depth limit for EAN 40 is 99 FSW. All times are in minutes. Times are for single dives, based on U.S. Navy Dive Tables and NOAA Nitrox Tables.**

Note that most dive computers provide single dive times that are much shorter, but have the capability to compute a multi-level dive, taking into account time spent at progressively shallower depths. Consequently, the time permitted by a dive computer on a single, non-repetitive dive is usually longer than what a table would allow, provided that you do not spend your entire time at the maximum depth of the dive. Nitrox dive computers, and dive computers in general, are a much more convenient, and usually more accurate way to compute depth and time.

Most dive computers will need to be set to nitrox and have the correct mixture and PO$_2$ entered before you start your dive.

©AquaLung. All rights reserved.

Recommended Surface Intervals for Nitrox Divers

The minimum recommended surface interval for divers using nitrox is 30 minutes, although a 60-minute interval is preferred. After long dives/extended exposures, a two-hour (120-minute) surface interval is recommended.

The minimum recommended surface interval is 30 minutes, but one hour is preferred. According to this computer, the diver needs to wait at least four more minutes before entering the water.

© Dive-Rite. All rights reserved.

Fire and Explosion Risks

If you've heard anything about nitrox, you've probably heard that there are fire and explosion risks when you use gas mixtures that have oxygen levels higher than 21%. Mixtures containing 40% or less oxygen are not considered at risk. This is a valid concern only for gas mixtures containing 41% or more oxygen.

Gas mixtures containing 41% or more oxygen are susceptible to fire and explosion if improperly handled. When high-pressure oxygen comes into contact with hydrocarbons, such as oil, the potential for fire and explosion is very real. Oxygen fueled fires are swift and usually difficult to extinguish.

Some diving equipment manufacturers insist that your equipment must be specially cleaned for oxygen service and use oxygen compatible seals and components. If you buy this type of equipment you must comply with the

If you are diving with gas mixtures that contain more than 40% oxygen, only the first stage of your regulator must be oxygen compatible.

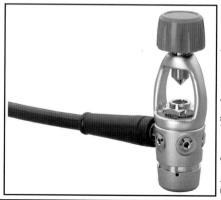

©AquaLung. All rights reserved.

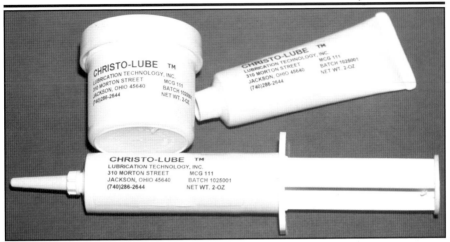

Only oxygen-safe lubricants may be used with gas mixtures containing more than 40% oxygen

manufacturer's conditions or the warranty on your equipment may be void.

Oxygen cleaning must be performed by a trained technician in a clean environment, using cleaning agents that have been deemed "safe" for this application. Oxygen compatible o-rings and regulator seats are available for many, but not all regulators. Special oxygen safe lubricants must be used in any equipment that is to be used with oxygen rich mixtures.

If you think that you will continue to dive with nitrox, and there is a chance that you will continue your training to dive with oxygen mixtures containing 41% oxygen or higher, you may want to consider purchasing dive gear designed for oxygen service. If after this course, you only dive with nitrox, this may be a good move.

If you purchase gear designed for oxygen service, such as a tank or regulator, and use it with systems that are not "oxygen clean," the gear must be considered "contaminated" and not used with mixtures containing 41% or higher oxygen until it has been cleaned again. For this reason, if you loan your nitrox compatible diving gear to another nitrox diver, you must be sure that they understand that they can only use it with gases and systems that are oxygen clean.

If you only dive with EAN 40 or less, oxygen compatible gear, oxygen cleaning, fires, and explosions are not things you need to be concerned about.

Scuba I.Q. Review

Do you understand the risks in nitrox diving? Do you know how to minimize these risks? Review these questions with your instructor.

1) The word CONVENTID is an acronym that stands for a series of words. List the words that CONVENTID represents.

2) Define the term "oxygen poisoning."

3) List two additional factors that may make you sensitive to oxygen toxicity.

4) List three precautions to help avoid oxygen toxicity while using EAN 32.

5) List the two gases that a nitrox diving computer takes into consideration when computing your allowable bottom time.

6) State the minimum recommended and preferred surface intervals when diving with nitrox.

7) State the recommended surface interval after extended dives with nitrox.

8) State the oxygen percentage in a nitrox mixture above which oxygen cleaning is considered essential.

9) State the conditions that must be met for equipment to be considered oxygen "safe."

Notes:

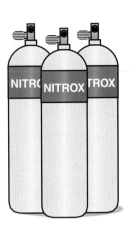

Chapter 4
Selecting Equipment for
Nitrox Diving

If you already own your own dive gear, you can dive with nitrox mixtures containing 40% oxygen or less without purchasing any additional equipment beyond that which you already own. However, you won't be able to take full advantage of the benefits of nitrox diving unless you use a nitrox dive computer.

In this chapter, we'll take a look at some minor gear modifications that you'll need to make as well as your choices if you decide to purchase dedicated nitrox diving gear.

Tank Marking and Identification

Any time you fill a tank with nitrox it must be identified as such. This will help to prevent accidents in the event that someone uses a tank filled with nitrox without taking the proper precautions.

The industry standard for tanks filled with nitrox is to mark the tank with both a "tank decal," as well as to identify the mixture with a label or tag. Nitrox tank wrap is a sticky backed tape, usually 4 or 5 inches wide, that is designed to completely encircle the diameter of the tank. The tape is usually printed in yellow with bold green letters with the word "NITROX" printed continuously on it. This tape makes it quick and easy to spot a nitrox bottle in a group of tanks.

Any tank used for nitrox diving must also have a tag or label attached to it where the exact nitrox mixture used in the tank can be read. Some shops use plastic tags that can be written on and reused, while others use labels stuck to the tank itself. It doesn't matter which style of marking device is used as long as the information is instantly available on the tank.

Any tank used for nitrox diving should have a tank wrap decal like this one on it.

TECHNICAL DIVING INTERNATIONAL CONTENTS LABEL	
OXYGEN%	
NITROGEN%	
HELIUM%	
OTHER	
MOD	/PO2
FACILITY	
INITIALS	
DATE	

WARNING
This Cylinder May Contain Mixtures Other Than Air. Proper Training And Analyzing Are Required To Use.

The contents of your tank must be clearly marked so that you know what is in it. The contents tag can be a hang tag or a decal.

Regulators Designed for Nitrox Service

As we've already mentioned, it is not essential to buy a special regulator if you only plan to dive with mixtures containing 40% oxygen or less. Almost any regulator you already own can be used for this type of service with no special modifications or cleaning, although some manufacturers may void a warranty when a regulator not designed for nitrox service is used with nitrox. Check with your instructor or dive store before you start to use an existing regulator with enriched air mixtures.

Many diving equipment manufacturers now sell regulators specifically designed for nitrox service. These regulators can usually be identified by yellow and/or green rings on the first stage and by yellow and/or green second stages. Nitrox regulators have special o-rings, nitrox compatible seats, and use special lubricants.

You may already own a regulator that can be converted to nitrox service if you decide that you need this capability and in the future, you intend to dive with mixtures that contain more than 40% oxygen.

In addition to the markings that are used on regulators specifically designed for nitrox service, you may also want to purchase a plastic hose wrap, designed to cover the low pressure hose connecting the first and second stages of your regulator. This is an additional method of identifying a regulator that will be used especially for nitrox service.

Remember that if you purchase a regulator specifically for nitrox you must not use it with any cylinders that have not been cleaned for oxygen service and filled at an oxygen safe facility. Use with anything but oxygen safe gas mixtures will expose the regulator to oils and contaminants that can lead to an oxygen fire or explosion. An oxygen fire could be fatal to you or anyone close by you.

Never use a regulator dedicated to nitrox service with anything but cylinders that have been cleaned for oxygen service.

©Scubapro. All rights reserved.

Dive Computers

Almost every manufacturer today offers nitrox dive computers for sale and there are many different models. Of course, you can use your air diving computer with nitrox, but you lose the advantage of the additional bottom time provided by using enriched air. In addition, air diving computers do not track your exposure to oxygen.

Most dedicated nitrox computers simultaneously track and display your nitrogen absorption for decompression calculations and your oxygen exposure. If you are making multiple deep dives in a single day, this type of information is extremely important.

If you decide to continue your diving education and obtain advanced nitrox certification, you'll definitely want a nitrox dive computer. Some of the more sophisticated models even allow you to change gas mixtures while diving, a technique used by many technical divers who switch to mixtures containing higher percentages of oxygen for decompression.

Most nitrox dive computers allow you to set the percentage of oxygen in your breathing mix anywhere between 21% and 50% oxygen. Some will even allow richer mixtures. However, most require that the percentage of oxygen in the mixture be set **before** you enter the water. This procedure must be

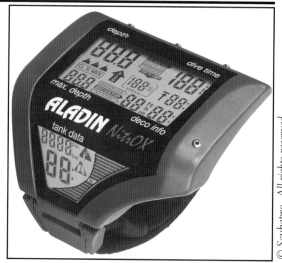

Most nitrox dive computers must be set for the mixture you are using before you enter the water.

© Scubapro. All rights reserved.

done prior to the start of every dive.

Some nitrox dive computers will default to 21% oxygen (air) when they are first "booted up" at the start of a dive day. Others will retain whatever mixture at which you set them. Whatever type of computer you use, it is essential that you verify that your computer is properly set for the mixture you will be using before each dive. This is essential for the computer to calculate your decompression and oxygen exposure properly. In most other ways, nitrox dive computers do not differ from air diving computers. They provide the same type of dive planning, repetitive dive calculations, and log functions. Dive computer models change regularly, so be sure to have your instructor show you what models are currently available and explain your choices to you.

In addition to programming your computer with the information on the mixture you will be using, you will also need to program it with the maximum partial pressure to which you are willing to expose yourself. To get the maximum depth capability from any nitrox mixture, you need to program your computer for a partial pressure of oxygen of 1.6. If you want to be more conservative, you can set your dive computer for a PO_2 of 1.4 or 1.5.

Whatever type of dive computer you use, it is essential for you to read the manual provided with it and to thoroughly understand how the computer should be used. If you rent a computer from a dive store, be sure to ask them to provide you with a copy of the manual, or at the very least, have them explain the computer's functions to you.

It's important to remember that none of the dive computers currently available provide an exact measurement of the nitrogen and oxygen levels inside your body. The computer only provides a mathematical model of what diving physiologists think is going on. Even if you follow your dive computer exactly, it's still possible to experience decompression sickness or oxygen toxicity. The same risks apply to using dive tables, with the added risk that you can make mistakes in your calculations.

Always be sure to set your computer for the percentage of oxygen in the mix, and the partial pressure of oxygen (PO_2).

Thermal Protection is Needed for Longer Dives

To get the full benefit of diving with nitrox, you'll need to be sure that you are wearing adequate thermal protection for the waters where you dive. Whether you dive in the tropics or in colder waters, the extended bottom times provided by nitrox will usually necessitate more thermal protection/insulation than what you might ordinarily wear.

While you might be able to dive in the Caribbean wearing a dive skin for short duration dives, if you use nitrox you'll probably need to consider wearing a tropical shorty wetsuit. The more diving you plan on doing, the more likely it is that you'll get cold, even in warmer waters.

To reap the maximum benefits of nitrox in waters colder than 65 degrees, you should consider a dry suit for optimal thermal protection. Dry suits are not difficult to use, but they do require additional training.

Oxygen Analyzer

Oxygen analyzers are electronic devices that are used to measure the percentage of oxygen in a gas mixture. They run on batteries and most are equipped with a "fuel cell" designed to record the percentage of oxygen in a gas mixture. Most modern oxygen analyzers have a digital display that shows the reading. All dive stores that fill nitrox cylinders have oxygen analyzers. They use them to check each cylinder after it has been filled to be sure that it contains the correct mixture of nitrogen and oxygen.

Oxygen analyzers are simple devices to use. Your instructor will show you how to use one during this course. In most cases, they require nothing more than to be turned on and allowed to stabilize while reading room air. After the analyzer has been on for a few minutes, it should read very close to 21% oxygen. If it does not, it is a simple matter to calibrate the analyzer to the correct reading, usually by turning a dial located on the front of the unit.

Once the analyzer has been calibrated it is connected to your cylinder using some type of device that will restrict the flow of nitrox to the analyzer so it is not exposed to high pressure. Once the nitrox is flowing steadily to the analyzer, and the reading has stabilized, the reading is noted.

Oxygen analyzers are simple devices to use. You will have the opportunity to use one during this course. Although there are several different manufacturers of analyzers with different designs, most models function in a similar manner.

It isn't necessary to purchase your own oxygen analyzer, although most serious nitrox divers end up purchasing their own units for use at home or on dive trips. An analyzer is especially useful for technical divers who own more than one nitrox cylinder and have them filled with different mixtures. In the event a tag is lost or falls off, it is a simple matter to analyze your own cylinder, rather than make a trip to the dive store for analysis. You must always know what gas mixture is in your cylinder.

Equipment that Doesn't Need to be Oxygen Clean

Equipment that is exposed to low pressure oxygen, such as buoyancy compensators and their low pressure inflators, dry suit inflation valves and regulator second stages, do not need to be cleaned or lubricated for oxygen service. There is no explosion or fire danger with any gear that is exposed to low pressure oxygen.

Buoyancy compensators and other low pressure devices do not need to be cleaned for oxygen service.

© *Zeagle Systems, Inc. All rights reserved.*

Scuba I.Q. Review

Are you ready to pick out your nitrox diving computer? Do you need a dedicated nitrox regulator? Discuss these issues with your instructor.

1) Describe the appearance of nitrox tank wrap used to identify nitrox cylinders.

2) Explain the purpose of a nitrox fill tag or label.

3) List the changes that must be made to a regulator to prepare a regulator for use with nitrox mixtures that do not exceed 40% oxygen.

4) List the three changes that must be made to a regulator to prepare it for nitrox service with gas mixtures containing more than 40% oxygen.

5) State the two factors for which your nitrox dive computer must be adjusted prior to every dive.

6) Explain why you may need additional thermal protection for nitrox diving.

7) Define the term "oxygen analyzer."

8) State the gas mixture that is most commonly used to calibrate an oxygen analyzer.

9) List two items of equipment that do not need to be cleaned for oxygen service.

Notes:

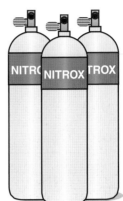

Chapter 5
Filling Your Cylinders for
Nitrox Diving

When you're getting ready to go nitrox diving, you must take your cylinders to a dive store that provides nitrox "fills." In this chapter, we'll discuss how to make sure you get the right gas mixture for your diving.

Selecting Your Mixture

To select your gas mixture, you must give some thought about where you will be diving at the time your tank is filled. If you plan to dive shallower than 100 feet, pick EAN 40 as this will give you the most bottom time. If you want to dive to depths down to 132 FSW, pick EAN 32.

With the versatility of EAN 32 you can dive at any depth within the traditional sport diving range. With other mixtures, you must know where you will dive and your planned depth when you take your cylinders to be filled.

The Blender

To most people, a blender is a kitchen appliance used to make milkshakes or frozen margaritas. To the nitrox diver, "the blender" is an important person who holds the key to your nitrox diving. Without a properly trained blender, you won't be able to dive nitrox with any degree of confidence.

In nitrox diving terms, a blender is a person who has specialized training and skill to fill nitrox diving cylinders with the exact gas that you need for your planned dive. The blender is almost always a highly skilled and avid nitrox diver himself. Blenders must take a specialized course in blending and must demonstrate that they are competent in their role prior to receiving their certification.

The blender's job is to supply you with the gas that you ask for when you present your tank to be filled. To this end, the blender makes the required calculations for the cylinder pressure and mixture that you need.

From a practical standpoint, although we would ideally like to have the

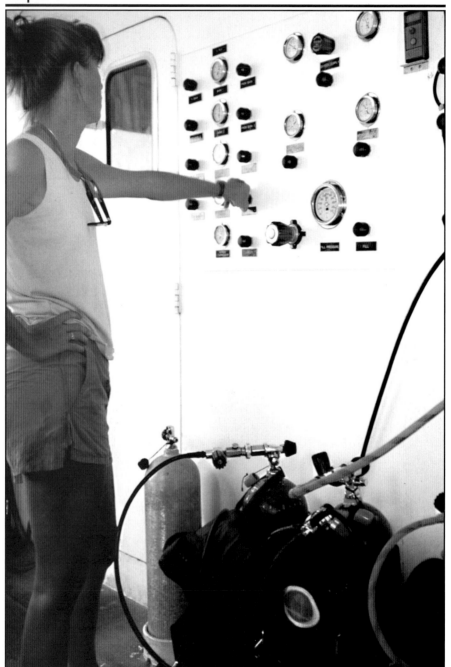

The nitrox blender must be trained and knowledgeable in their job. It's their job to make sure you get the mixture you request.

Every blender must complete a training course to ensure that they have the capability to fill nitrox cylinders correctly.

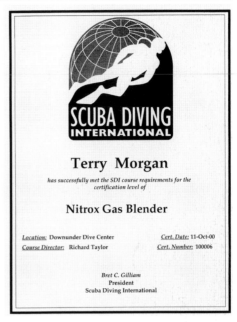

SCUBA DIVING
INTERNATIONAL

Terry Morgan

has successfully met the SDI course requirements for the certification level of

Nitrox Gas Blender

Location: Downunder Dive Center   *Cert. Date:* 11-Oct-00
Course Director: Richard Taylor   *Cert. Number:* 100006

Bret C. Gilliam
President
Scuba Diving International

exact gas mixture we request, this is not always possible, due to errors in gauges and other factors. For this reason, it is a generally accepted industry standard that as long as the mixture in your tank is within 1% of the target mix, this is sufficient. Given this standard, when you specify EAN 32 you may end up with either 31% oxygen or 33% oxygen. Both of these mixtures are still considered within acceptable limits. If you ask for EAN 40, and your gear is not cleaned for oxygen service, the blender will be conservative to ensure that you do not end up with a mixture that exceeds 40% oxygen.

The Nitrox Filling Station

There are a number of different types of filling stations that dive stores use for filling nitrox cylinders. Some systems are more sophisticated than others, and some have wider capabilities than others do.

It is not essential for you to know the exact methods used to fill nitrox cylinders, or the terminology that describes each technique. However, if you have dedicated nitrox equipment, i.e, an oxygen clean regulator or cylinders, your cylinders should only be filled at a fill station that is an oxygen clean facility. Anything less will contaminate your equipment with oils that could lead to an explosion or fire if you later use your equipment with nitrox mixtures containing greater than 40% oxygen.

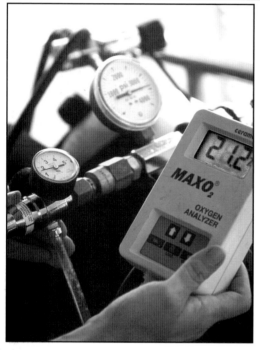

The mixture in your tank should be within 1% of the percentage that you request. Be sure to allow time for the analyzer to stabilize before taking a reading.

How do you know whether or not a nitrox filling station is oxygen clean? Ask! Don't assume that all filling stations are oxygen clean. One way that you'll know for sure is whether the station can fill nitrox mixtures containing more than 40% oxygen. If they have this capability, then their system must be oxygen clean.

Depending upon the type of filling system in use, the blender may start out by partially filling your cylinder with pure oxygen and then topping off the cylinder with air. Other systems use a semi-permeable membrane, which acts like a filter, to separate nitrogen from oxygen and achieve the gas mixture you desire. Whatever method is used to fill your tank is acceptable provided you get the correct gas mixture (as long as your system does not need to be oxygen clean).

Signs and labels on the equipment normally identify nitrox filling stations. In addition, the blender's certification is usually displayed near the fill station, too. If you have any uncertainties about the capabilities of the fill station, ask questions before they fill your tank.

To allow enough time to properly fill a nitrox cylinder, you may want to drop your cylinders off and pick them up later in the day. Most dive stores will request that you leave your cylinders with them for nitrox filling. If you're going to be in a hurry, you may be unable to get your tanks filled exactly when you need them unless you have made prior arrangements.

You may need to drop your nitrox cylinders off to be filled and pick them up at a later time.

Analyzing Your Breathing Gas

Once your tank has been filled, the blender will either check the mixture in your cylinder for you, or have you check the mixture yourself. Either method is acceptable, provided you are satisfied that you have the correct gas mixture in your cylinder.

With the oxygen analyzer properly calibrated and the gas flowing from the cylinder, the analyzer should respond to the gas mixture very quickly. Just as it takes a minute or two for the analyzer to stabilize during calibration, it may take a minute for the analyzer to stabilize while taking a reading. You will not get an instantaneous reading of the correct amount.

If the blender allows you to analyze your own gas, but you don't recall exactly how to adjust the analyzer, be sure to ask the blender to show you how it is done. Oxygen analyzers are delicate instruments and careless handling can damage them very quickly.

Whether the blender analyzes the gas or you do it yourself, the blender will ask you to sign your name in a log indicating that your tanks have been filled, as well as the date, the gas mixture, your certification number, and the pressure in the cylinder. Your signature indicates that you take responsibility for the nitrox that has been delivered to you, and that you are satisfied that your cylinders have been filled properly.

You will be required to fill out a nitrox log to ackowledge that you received a cylinder filled with a particular nitrox mixture.

Scuba I.Q. Review

When your tank is filled for nitrox diving, you must take an active role in ensuring you have the correct mixture for your diving. Discuss the following issues with your instructor and be sure you thoroughly understand the concepts presented in this chapter.

1) Define the term "blender" as it applies to nitrox diving.

2) State the maximum allowable range of gas mixtures that are acceptable when you specify EAN 32 for filling your cylinder.

3) Explain the steps used to analyze the nitrox mixture in a diving cylinder.

4) List the information that you will be required to supply when you sign the log accepting your nitrox fill.

Notes:

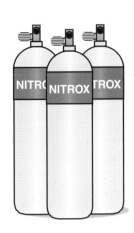

Chapter 6
Planning the Nitrox Dive

No matter what type of diving you do, it's always essential to plan your dive. In nitrox diving, your planning will be only slightly more involved. Planning for a nitrox dive should not take any more time, but it does require a bit of different thinking compared to planning for an air dive.

Check the Availability of Nitrox

If you're diving in your local area, you probably already know which dive stores and boats offer nitrox. However, if you are planning a trip outside of your area, and you want to dive nitrox, you'll need to do a bit of research before you travel if you want to ensure that nitrox is available.

Most popular dive magazines have directories in the back that list the stores in any given area that are nitrox providers. You can also search on the Internet.

Once you have located a store that fills nitrox cylinders, be sure to contact them to make sure that their system is operational and check what they charge for nitrox fills. Most stores charge by the percentage of oxygen included in the mixture. Tank fills that contain a higher percentage of oxygen typically cost more than those with a lower percentage.

Set Your Dive Computer

Prior to every nitrox dive, you must check your nitrox dive computer to be sure that it is properly set for the mixture you are using. There are two settings that you must make, one is for the percentage of oxygen that you will be using, and the other is for the maximum PO_2 to which you are willing to expose yourself.

Some dive computers, and the manuals that describe them, use the term "fraction of oxygen" or "FO_2" rather than the percentage of oxygen in the mix. The fraction of oxygen is the decimal equivalent of the percentage of oxygen in the mix. For example, 32% oxygen is the same thing as .32 FO_2.

Not all dive stores are capable of filling nitrox cylinders. Most Scuba Diving International stores will have this capability.

©2000 S. Barsky. All rights reserved.

Different dive computers have different default settings for both the oxygen percentage in the mix and the maximum PO$_2$. These default settings tend to be conservative. In most cases, the default setting for the percentage of oxygen will be 21%. The default setting for PO$_2$ is frequently 1.4. If you fail to change these settings you will not be getting the full benefit of the capabilities of your computer and nitrox.

Today there are numerous different types of dive computers on the market, so your instructor will show you the specific techniques for setting your dive computer. However, here are some general guidelines that you need to keep in mind.

Most modern dive computers can be set in 1% increments so that you can adjust the oxygen percentage to the exact mixture in your cylinder. In addition, the maximum PO$_2$ that most computers will allow is 1.6, although a few will allow higher settings.

If you set the oxygen percentage at the correct level for EAN 32, but accidentally set your computer to a higher PO$_2$, you will be exposing yourself to dangerous oxygen levels should you also exceed the maximum operating depth of 132 FSW for this mixture. Conversely, if you set your computer for EAN 32 but change the maximum PO$_2$ to less than 1.6, you will be restrict-

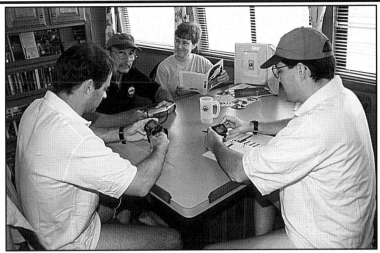

You and your dive partner need to be sure to set your computer prior to diving. It must be programmed for the correct percentage of oxygen and maximum PO₂.

ing your maximum depth, which may be desirable under certain conditions.

If you plan to use nitrox but intend to dive conservatively because you are concerned about decompression sickness, you can use an air diving computer and follow its normal limits. If you are using a nitrox computer and want to follow air diving limits, set your oxygen percentage for 21% and your PO$_2$ for 1.6. However, you must still remember to faithfully observe the maximum operating depth for the mix.

Most dive computers will retain the settings that you make at the start of a day of diving for any subsequent dives, until you change the settings in the computer. However, some dive computers will default back to air (21% oxygen) once the computer shuts down. It is also possible, that your computer could be accidentally reset to a different gas mixture or partial pressure through contact with other equipment. In addition, more sophisticated computers allow users to change gas mixtures for decompression. For these reasons, it is always wise to recheck the settings on your computer prior to each dive.

If it has been awhile since you last used your dive computer, take the time to re-read the manual so you remember how to use it properly. Have the computer with you when you read the manual so you can review any procedures you might have forgotten. Most dive computers have more features than the average diver will use. It is easy to forget how to make some of the more obscure settings. If you are going on an extended dive trip, such as a tropical dive vacation, be sure to take the manual with you, or at the very least, any "cue" cards supplied by the manufacturer.

Maximum Depth Alarm

If your computer is equipped with a maximum depth alarm, you should set this for the MOD of 132 feet of sea water when diving with EAN 32. Set your alarm for the appropriate depth with other mixtures. This will help you to avoid violating your maximum operating depth should you become distracted while taking photos or engaged in some other activity.

Plan Your Maximum Depth and Bottom Time

Use the planning function on your dive computer to scroll through the allowable bottom times for each 10-foot increment in your depth, down to 130 feet of seawater. If you are on the surface, between dives, use the planning function of your dive computer to check on how long you need to spend on the surface between dives to make the next dive that you want to do.

Remember, the minimum surface interval you should spend on the surface between nitrox dives is 30 minutes, and a surface interval of one hour is recommended. Following extended dives, longer surface intervals are recommended.

Most computers have a planning and/or simulation function so you can calculate your allowable bottom time and surface intervals.

© AquaLung. All rights reserved.

Nitrox Dive Tables

There are nitrox dive tables that can be used to plan and make nitrox dives. These tables are similar to the air diving tables you may have seen in the past.

Keep in mind that the nitrox no-decompression limits used by dive tables are for single depth, i.e., "square profile" dives. If you compare dive times listed in any nitrox dive table to your dive computer's times, your computer will be more conservative for single depth dives. However, your computer calculates multi-level dives automatically for you "on-the-fly", something that is difficult to do with dive tables, ultimately allowing for longer total bottom times.

Start your dive computer. Compare the scrolling dive times it displays for the no-decompression limits for EAN 32, or other mixtures, to this table.

Plan Your Dive Conservatively

For dives that are cold or strenuous, avoid diving to the maximum operating depth and shorten your bottom time, or both. Even if you use your dive computer exactly the way it was designed to be used, there is always a slight risk of decompression sickness.

Plan Your Dive With Your Buddy

Your buddy should be diving with the same nitrox mixture that you are using. If your dive buddy fills his tank with air, or a different nitrox mixture, and dives beyond the maximum operating depth for the mixture you are using, you will not be able to go to his aid if he needs help. If you violate the maximum operating depth of your mixture in a stressful situation there is a high risk that you could suffer from oxygen toxicity.

Plan Your Activity

Before you enter the water, you should know your planned activity for the dive as well as the route you plan for the dive. Remember that exertion can be a triggering factor in oxygen toxicity at the maximum operating depth. Avoid dives where you will be required to swim against strong currents or otherwise must exert yourself heavily.

Your activity should be planned prior to the dive. Underwater photographers appreciate the longer bottom times provided by nitrox.

Plan for a Precautionary Decompression Stop

You should plan to make a precautionary decompression stop (safety stop) at the end of every dive. Always plan to leave yourself enough nitrox to make a stop at a depth of 10-15 feet for 3-5 minutes at the end of each dive. Discuss how and where you will make your safety stop with your dive partner.

Planning for Emergencies

As in all diving, you should always know how to summon assistance if a diving accident should occur. If you are diving from the beach, know the location of the nearest telephone and what number you should call in the event of an emergency. If you have a cellular phone in your car, be sure that you check the signal strength before you dive to ensure you can dial out if this is the device you are depending on to summon help.

On charter boats, the captain will normally have a marine radio to summon assistance in an emergency. If you are diving from a private boat, it should be equipped with either a fixed or handheld marine radio to use to summon help on Channel 16.

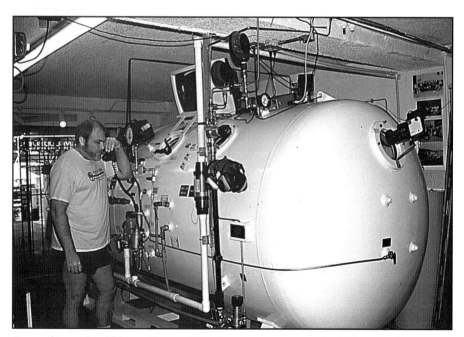

Every divers should have dive accident insurance to cover the high cost of treatment in a recompression chamber.

In all pressure related diving injuries (decompression sickness and lung over-pressure injuries), once you have established a means of evacuation for the injured diver, your second call should be to the Divers Alert Network (DAN) at 919-684-8111. This 24-hour number will accept collect calls. DAN's trained medical staff will direct you to the nearest recompression chamber for treatment, if necessary. It is strongly recommended that every diver have diving accident insurance to cover the high cost of recompression treatment if it should ever become necessary.

Scuba I.Q. Review

Use this chapter as the basis for a discussion with your instructor to help plan your dive.

1) List two ways that you can check for nitrox availability at your destination when planning a dive trip.

2) State the two settings that must be checked and/or adjusted on your nitrox dive computer prior to every dive.

3) State the most common default setting and the preferred setting for PO2 on most dive computers.

4) State the most common default setting for the percentage of oxygen in the mix on most dive computers.

5) Demonstrate the procedure for using the planning function on your dive computer to check the maximum time you can spend at a depth of 100 feet using EAN 32.

6) Explain why it is important for both you and your dive partner to be using the same nitrox mixture rather than allowing one member of the dive team to use air or a different nitrox mixture.

SCUBA DIVING
INTERNATIONAL

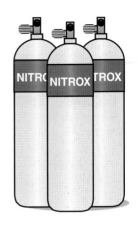

Chapter 7
Making Nitrox Dives

For all practical purposes, making a dive with nitrox is no different than making a dive with ordinary compressed air, other than the depth limitations for mixtures containing a higher percentage of oxygen than EAN 32. You won't feel any different and you usually won't need to change the way you dive.

Descent

If you are diving in a location that you've been to before, and you know the depth to the bottom, you do not need to monitor your depth too closely as you descend. However, if you are diving in an unfamiliar location, or at a deep spot where the possibility exists to exceed your maximum operating depth, be sure to closely monitor your computer as you descend, and control your buoyancy. Do not exceed the maximum operating depth for the particular mixture you are using.

Although most computers will sound an alarm if you exceed the maximum operating depth for your mix, not all alarms are sufficiently loud, especially if you are wearing a wetsuit hood or suffer from any hearing loss. You must also visually check your computer as you descend and periodically monitor it throughout your dive.

Watch Your Bottom Time!

During the dive, your nitrox computer will display your running bottom time, your maximum depth, your current depth, and your oxygen time limit, which will usually be displayed as a percentage. You must monitor both your allowable remaining bottom time to avoid decompression and exceeding your oxygen time limit. You will need to ascend when your allowable remaining bottom time approaches 10 (ten) minutes, or when your oxygen time limit approaches 90%, whichever occurs first.

If you dive prudently, in most sport diving situations, you will probably never reach either your no decompression limit or your oxygen time limit.

Watch your bottom time carefully whenever you dive.

On no-decompression dives, it is virtually impossible to obtain an oxygen exposure of more than 45%-50%.

If you are making a dive right at the maximum operating depth for your mix, be sure to monitor yourself for any effects of oxygen toxicity. If you experience any of the symptoms described earlier in this book, you should immediately ascend to a shallower depth. Your ascent rate should be normal; you should not make a rapid ascent.

Ascending at the End of Your Dive

As your nitrox supply diminishes you should be preparing to leave the bottom. On dives in shallow water, you should be leaving the bottom with a minimum of 500 p.s.i. of remaining air pressure in your cylinder. On deeper dives, or if you have a high air consumption rate, you should be leaving the bottom with a minimum of 750 p.s.i. in your cylinder.

Ascend at the rate prescribed by your dive computer and carefully control your buoyancy as you ascend. Monitor your computer continuously as you ascend and be prepared to halt your ascent if you find you are ascending too fast.

Be sure to make a precautionary decompression stop (safety stop) at a depth of 10-15 feet for 3-5 minutes at the end of your dive. This will help prevent, but cannot ensure, that you will avoid decompression sickness.

During Your Surface Interval

During your surface interval you should relax, rewarm if you became cold during the dive, and drink fluids free of caffeine and alcohol. Use the planning function of your dive computer to check your allowable bottom time for the next dive you intend to do. Allow yourself sufficient time to prepare your gear and check your dive computer to be sure that it is set for the correct mixture and PO_2.

Maximum Exposure to Nitrox

The maximum exposure to any nitrox mixture at its maximum operating depth must not exceed 45 minutes on a single dive or a total of 150 minutes in any 24-hour period. From a practical sport diving standpoint it would be difficult to put in this type of bottom time over a series of dives at these depths in most situations due to fatigue, the limitations of most diving service providers, and decompression limitations.

This limitation is based on an exposure to a PO_2 of 1.6. Much longer exposures are possible at shallower depths. Your dive computer will calculate this exposure for you.

Emergency Procedures

In the rare event that you or your dive buddy experience any of the symptoms of oxygen toxicity, it is essential that you begin a deliberate ascent to a shallower depth. While the risk of oxygen toxicity while diving with nitrox is low, it is a real risk.

If your dive partner experiences a convulsion while at depth, the only thing that you can do is to try to get him back to the surface quickly. In most cases when a diver convulses underwater, drowning is the end result because they are unable to hold the regulator in their mouth, and water inhalation almost always occurs. This is usually fatal.

Decompression sickness is always a possibility whenever you dive, and nitrox diving is no exception. There is no difference in the treatment of decompression sickness for the nitrox diver.

Any diver who is on the surface and suffering from either decompression sickness or a lung over-pressure injury should be placed on 100% oxygen immediately and transported to the nearest recompression chamber. Contact the Divers Alert Network for instructions on how and where to proceed for definitive treatment.

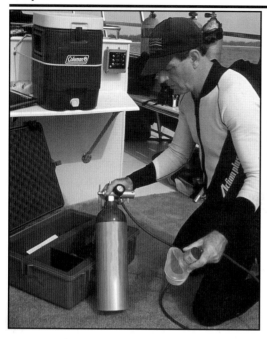

Pure oxygen is the recommended first aid for decompression sickness or lung over-pressure injuries that occur as a result of a nitrox dive.

All other emergency procedures, such as out-of-breathing gas emergencies are handled just as you would handle them when diving with ordinary air.

Log Your Dive

Be sure to log your dives as soon as possible after you're finished diving. If your dive computer has a download capability, this is a great way to record the details of your dive.

Scuba I.Q. Review

Discuss the procedures for nitrox diving completely with your instructor to be sure that you understand them correctly.

1) State the two types of alarms that most dive nitrox computers use to alert you when you are approaching your maximum operating depth for your gas mixture.

2) State the minimum time prior to reaching the no-decompression limit you should begin your ascent.

3) State the procedure you should follow if you begin to experience any symptoms of oxygen toxicity.

©Scubapro. All rights reserved.

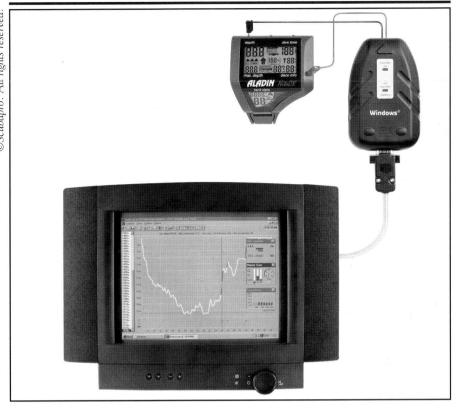

Most nitrox computers will allow you to download your dive log to a PC.

4) Demonstrate the procedure for using your dive computer to calculate your allowable bottom time for a repetitive dive following your first dive.

5) State the maximum total dive time you may have at a depth of 132 feet of seawater using EAN 32 in any single 24-hour period.

6) Explain why an oxygen convulsion is almost always fatal underwater.

7) State the first aid treatment for decompression sickness or a lung overpressure injury while using nitrox.

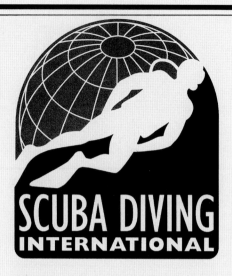

Jack Rice

has successfully met the SDI course requirements in the use of 22% to 40% nitrox mixtures to a maximum depth of 130 fsw/40 msw.

Nitrox Diver

Location: **Dive USA**

Course Director: **Brian Johnson**

Cert. Date: **11-Oct-00**

Cert. Number: **100000**

Bret C. Gilliam
President
Scuba Diving International

Upon successful completion of your nitrox course you will receive a wall certificate and certification card identifying you as a nitrox diver.

Notes:

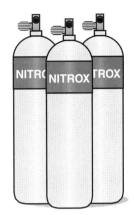

Chapter 8
Extending Your Nitrox Capabilities

Now that you've completed this course, you will be interested to know other ways that you can extend your nitrox capabilities. There is much more to nitrox than the mixtures we have covered in this book. For example, you can use an infinite variety of nitrox mixtures. You can use a nitrox rebreather, of which there are several different models. You can also learn to use multiple gas mixtures in a single dive and to use gas mixtures other than oxygen and nitrogen. All of these additional training courses are considered part of the specialty area of diving known as "technical diving."

Technical diving is a type of diving that goes beyond traditional sport diving. Typically, it requires additional specialized training, methods, and equipment. It provides the diver with capabilities beyond the limitations of sport diving.

The leader in technical diver training is Technical Diving International (TDI), sister company to Scuba Diving International. Technical Diving International offers courses in nitrox, advanced nitrox, semi-closed circuit rebreathers, fully closed-circuit rebreathers, and tri-mix. These courses all build on the information and techniques that you have learned during this course.

Advanced Nitrox Certification

In the SDI Easy Nitrox Diving Course you have just completed, you have learned how to use your dive computer to make dives using nitrox mixtures containing 40% oxygen or less. Because this course is specifically designed for divers using dive computers, the content has been structured to eliminate as much of the mathematical calculations and equation formulas as possible, since these functions are quite efficiently performed by the computer.

Within the TDI division, other nitrox certifications are available that will provide a more technical curriculum of academics, physiology, and math theory. The TDI Nitrox diver program is a more in-depth approach to the subject and teaches all relevant math equations to manually calculate Equivalent Air Depth (EAD), Maximum Operating Depth MOD) for a given mix, Partial Pressures, etc. as well as practical use of nitrox dive tables.

TDI Advanced Nitrox prepares and qualifies the diver to use mixes containing greater than 40% oxygen content and introduces the user to decompression procedures. Advanced Nitrox training qualifies you to use nitrox gas mixtures containing oxygen in any ratio with nitrogen and additionally includes use of 100% oxygen. With this course, your nitrox diving capabilities are complete.

Semi-Closed Circuit Rebreather Certification

Semi-closed circuit rebreathers are a specialized type of scuba gear that have become very popular with divers in recent years. The semi-closed circuit rebreather is designed to recirculate most of each breath you take, by removing the carbon dioxide (CO_2) from your exhaled breath and adding oxygen as it is consumed.

Semi-closed circuit rebreathers for recreational diving are designed to use nitrox as the breathing gas. They allow you to carry a much smaller cylinder of gas, yet greatly extend your bottom time. These are simple mechanical devices that are easy to learn to use.

Semi-closed circuit rebreathers are very popular with divers.

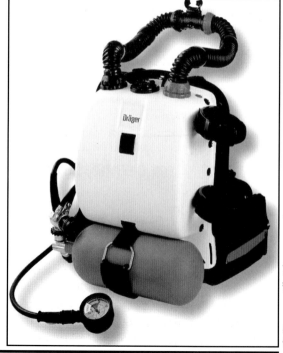

© Drager. All rights reserved.

There are many advantages to using a semi-closed circuit rebreather besides extended bottom time. If you dive from a small boat, using a semi-closed circuit rebreather will save a great deal of space in terms of the size and number of scuba cylinders you must take along to dive.

Another advantage of the semi-closed circuit rebreather is that they give off very few bubbles and are nearly silent, making it much easier to get closer to certain types of marine life. In addition, the chemical reaction that removes the carbon dioxide warms the breathing gas, helping to maintain body heat in colder waters.

Fully Closed-Circuit Rebreather Certification

Unlike the semi-closed circuit rebreather, fully closed-circuit models do not release any breathing gas bubbles into the water, except during the ascent at the end of the dive. They work in a similar manner to the semi-closed circuit rebreather.

There are two types of fully closed-circuit rebreathers; oxygen rebreathers and electronic mixed-gas rebreathers. Oxygen rebreathers use 100% oxygen and are only used by military divers for shallow water diving, down to depths of 25 feet. This type of rebreather is generally unavailable to the general public and impractical for most sport diving.

Fully-closed circuit electronic rebreathers are more complex than semi-closed circuit units and typically involve some type of on-board electronics to control the gas mixture that you breathe. These rebreathers require extensive training, but they have much broader capabilities, and may be used at extreme depths, hundreds of feet deep. They automatically mix oxygen and nitrogen, or other gas mixtures, to provide exactly the right amount of oxygen, regardless of your depth. They are also much more expensive to purchase, operate, and maintain than semi-closed circuit rebreathers.

Diving with a fully closed-circuit electronic rebreather is considered to be the most sophisticated type of diving that divers do today.

Tri-Mix Certification

Tri-mix is a gas mixture containing helium, nitrogen, and oxygen. This type of gas mixture is used for diving at depths deeper than 130 feet of seawater, down to 200 feet of seawater and beyond.

The concept behind tri-mix diving is that by replacing most of the nitrogen in the breathing gas with helium, you will be affected less by nitrogen narcosis than you would be using regular air. This is the reason why divers use tri-mix. Tri-mix is the type of gas mixture that commercial divers use when

Tri-mix divers must carry large quantities of breathing gas with them.

© OMS. All rights reserved.

working at depths down to 2000 feet of seawater.

Tri-mix diving is almost always decompression diving, which also requires additional training. Decompression diving involves increased risk.

Scuba I.Q. Review

As divers, there is always something new for us to learn. Discuss these technical diving courses with your instructor to gain a greater understanding of other activities you can pursue to build on your nitrox training.

1) Define the term "technical diving."

2) State the difference between the course you have just completed and advanced nitrox certification.

3) State the maximum percentage of oxygen that you will learn to use in an advanced nitrox diving course.

4) Define the term, "semi-closed circuit rebreather."

5) Define the term, "fully closed-circuit rebreather."

6) Define the term, "tri-mix" diving.

7) State the reason why divers use tri-mix breathing gas.

Additional Reading

Barsky, S. *Dry Suit Diving, 3rd Edition.* Hammerhead Press, Santa Barbara, CA, 1999, 185 pages

Beeson, H., Stewart, W., Woods, S. *Safe Use of Oxygen and Oxygen Systems,* ASTM, West Conshohocken, PA, 2000, 99 pages

Bove, A., Davis, J. *Diving Medicine,* 3rd Edition, W.B. Saunders,Philadelphia, PA, 1997, 418 pages

Gilliam, B. Von Maier, R., Crea, J. *Deep Diving: An Advanced Guide to Physiology, Procedures, and Systems.* Watersport Books, San Diego, CA, 1995, 352 pages

Lang, M. (Ed.) *DAN Nitrox Workshop Proceedings, Nov. 3-4, 2000.* Divers Alert Network, Durham, NC. 197 pages

Odom, J. *TDI Nitrox Manual,* Technical Diving International. Topsham, ME, 82 pages.

SDI Headquarters Message

When nitrox first came into widespread use by sport divers in the early 1990s, its use was frequently criticized by conservatives. In the ensuing debate, a considerable amount of incorrect and speculative information was circulated throughout the diving industry.

A historic conference of medical, scientific, research and operational experts was held November 3-4, 2000 to share hard data on the numbers of divers and instructors certified in nitrox, as well as information on nitrox diving accidents and the actual practices of sport divers who use nitrox. Conference attendees included representatives of the international dive training agencies, manufacturers, NOAA, U.S. Navy, DAN, scientific and university programs, commercial diving, resorts, liveaboard dive vessels, as well as research participants from various fields specializing in breathing gases and oxygen compatibility with diving equipment.

The findings of that conference are summarized below (excerpted from the Workshop Proceedings published in January 2001). It is interesting to note that every finding reflects the published recommendations and training practices as originally crafted by TDI and SDI since 1994. It is also worth noting that TDI has trained more divers and instructors in nitrox than any other agency in the world.

DAN Nitrox Workshop Recommendations

For entry level, recreational open-circuit nitrox diving:

• No evidence was presented that showed an increased risk of DCS from the use of oxygen enriched air (nitrox) versus compressed air.

• A maximum PO_2 of 1.6 atm was accepted based on its history of use and scientific studies.

• Routine CO_2 retention screening is not necessary.

• Oxygen analyzers should use a controlled-flow sampling device.

• Oxygen analysis of the breathing gas should be performed by the blender and/or dispenser and verified by the end user.

• Training agencies recognize the effectiveness of dive computers.

• For recreational diving, there is no need to track whole body exposure to oxygen (OUT/UPTD).

• Use of the "CNS Oxygen Clock" concept, based on NOAA oxygen exposure limits, should be taught. However, it should be noted that CNS Oxygen toxicity could occur suddenly and unexpectedly.

• No evidence was presented, based on history of use, to show an unreasonable risk of fire or ignition when using up to 40% oxygen nitrox with standard scuba equipment. The level of risk is related to specific equipment configurations and the user should rely on the manufacturer's recommendations.

Equivalent Air Depths - Imperial (Feet of Seawater)

Air Table	.21	.22	.23	.24	.25	.26	.27	.28	.29	.30	.31	.32	.33	.34	.35	.36	.37	.38	.39	.40
30	30	30	31	32	33	34	35	36	37	38	39	40	41	42	43	44	46	47	48	49
40	40	40	41	42	43	44	46	47	48	49	50	51	53	54	55	57	58	60	61	63
50	50	51	52	53	54	55	56	58	59	60	62	63	64	66	67	69	71	72	74	76
60	60	61	62	63	64	66	67	69	70	71	73	75	76	78	80	81	83	85	87	89
70	70	71	72	74	75	76	78	80	81	83	84	86	88	90	92	94	96	98	100	102
80	80	81	82	84	86	87	89	90	92	94	96	98	100	102	104	106	108	110	113	
90	90	91	93	94	96	98	100	101	103	105	107	109	112	114	116	118	121			
100	100	101	103	105	107	108	110	112	114	117	119	121	123	126	128					
110	110	111	113	115	117	119	121	123	126	128	130	133	135							
120	120	121	123	126	128	130	132	134	137	139	142									
130	130	132	134	136	138	141	143	145	148	150										
140	140	142	144	146	149	151	154	156	159											
MOD																				
1.4	187	177	167	159	151	144	138	132	126	121	116	111	107	102	99	95	91	88	85	82
1.6	218	207	196	187	178	170	162	155	149	143	137	132	127	122	117	113	109	105	102	99

How To Use this Table: Be sure to use a straight edge, such as a ruler or sheet of paper to align the rows and columns to avoid making mistakes in the use of this table. Find the percentage of oxygen in your mixture in the top row, reading from right to left. Read down that column until you find your planned maximum depth. Read across the row to the left. The number in the column at the far left is your equivalent air depth for the mixture you are using. To find your Maximum Operating Depth for the mixture you are using, find the row with the percentage of oxygen in your mixture. read down the column until you get to the bottom row of the table. This is your MOD for this mixture.

Depth, Mix and PO₂ Chart - Imperial (Feet of Seawater)

PO2	O2 Time	.21	.22	.23	.24	.25	.26	.27	.28	.29	.30	.31	.32	.33	.34	.35	.36	.37	.38	.39	.40
1.0	300	124	117	110	104	99	93	89	84	80	77	73	70	67	64	61	58	56	53	51	49
1.1	240	139	132	124	118	112	106	101	96	92	88	84	80	77	73	70	67	65	62	60	57
1.2	210	155	147	139	132	125	119	113	108	103	99	94	90	87	83	80	77	74	71	68	66
1.3	180	171	162	153	145	138	132	125	120	114	110	105	101	97	93	89	86	82	79	77	74
1.4	150	187	177	167	159	151	144	138	132	126	121	116	111	107	102	99	95	91	88	85	82
1.5	120	202	192	182	173	165	157	150	143	137	132	126	121	117	112	108	104	100	97	93	90
1.6	45	218	207	196	187	178	170	162	155	149	143	137	132	127	122	117	113	109	105	102	99

How to Use this Table: This table provides the maximum allowable oxygen exposures for different oxygen mixtures at PO₂s up to 1.6. The left hand column shows the PO₂ values. The next column to the right shows oxygen exposures in minutes. Each of the columns for PO₂ values list the depths at which the mixture in that column reaches a range of PO₂ values from 1.0 to 1.6.

Example: With a PO₂ of 1.6, how long can you spend at 113 feet breathing EAN 36? Answer: 45 minutes.

Equivalent Air Depths - Metric

Depth	21%	22%	23%	24%	25%	26%	27%	28%	29%	30%	31%	32%	33%	34%	35%	36%	37%	38%	39%	40%
10	10	10	9	9	9	9	8	8	8	8	7	7	7	7	6	6	6	6	5	5
11	11	11	10	10	10	10	9	9	9	9	8	8	8	8	7	7	7	6	6	6
12	12	12	11	11	11	11	10	10	10	9	9	9	9	8	8	8	8	7	7	7
13	13	13	12	12	12	12	11	11	11	10	10	10	10	9	9	9	8	8	8	7
14	14	14	13	13	13	12	12	12	12	11	11	11	10	10	10	9	9	9	9	8
15	15	15	14	14	14	13	13	13	12	12	12	12	11	11	11	10	10	10	9	9
16	16	16	15	15	15	14	14	14	13	13	13	12	12	12	11	11	11	10	10	10
17	17	17	16	16	16	15	15	15	14	14	14	13	13	13	12	12	12	11	11	11
18	18	18	17	17	17	16	16	16	15	15	14	14	14	13	13	13	12	12	12	11
19	19	19	18	18	18	17	17	16	16	16	15	15	15	14	14	13	13	13	12	12
20	20	20	19	19	18	18	18	17	17	17	16	16	15	15	15	14	14	14	13	13
21	21	21	20	20	19	19	19	18	18	17	17	17	16	16	16	15	15	14	14	14
22	22	22	21	21	20	20	20	19	19	18	18	18	17	17	16	16	16	15	15	14
23	23	23	22	22	21	21	20	20	20	19	19	18	18	18	17	17	16	16	15	15
24	24	24	23	23	22	22	21	21	21	20	20	19	19	18	18	18	17	17	16	16
25	25	25	24	24	23	23	22	22	21	21	21	20	20	19	19	18	18	17	17	17
26	26	26	25	25	24	24	23	23	22	22	21	21	21	20	20	19	19	18	18	17
27	27	27	26	26	25	25	24	24	23	23	22	22	21	21	20	20	20	19	19	18
28	28	28	27	27	26	26	25	25	24	24	23	23	22	22	21	21	20	20	19	19
29	29	29	28	28	27	27	26	26	25	25	24	24	23	23	22	22	21	21	20	20
30	30	29	29	28	28	27	27	26	26	25	25	24	24	23	23	22	22	21	21	20
31	31	30	30	29	29	28	28	27	27	26	26	25	25	24	24	23	23	22	22	
32	32	31	31	30	30	29	29	28	28	27	27	26	26	25	25	24	23	23		
33	33	32	32	31	31	30	30	29	29	28	28	27	26	26	25	25	24			
34	34	33	33	32	32	31	31	30	30	29	28	28	27	27	26	26				
35	35	34	34	33	33	32	32	31	30	30	29	29	28	28	27					

Depth	21%	22%	23%	24%	25%	26%	27%	28%	29%	30%	31%	32%	33%	34%	35%	36%	37%	38%	39%	40%
36	0.97	1.01	1.06	1.10	1.15	1.20	1.24	1.29	1.33	1.38	1.43	1.47	1.52	1.56	1.61					
37	0.99	1.03	1.08	1.13	1.18	1.22	1.27	1.32	1.36	1.41	1.46	1.50	1.55	1.60						
38	1.01	1.06	1.10	1.15	1.20	1.25	1.30	1.34	1.39	1.44	1.49	1.54	1.58							
39	1.03	1.08	1.13	1.18	1.23	1.27	1.32	1.37	1.42	1.47	1.52	1.57								
40	1.05	1.10	1.15	1.20	1.25	1.30	1.35	1.40	1.45	1.50	1.55	1.60								
41	1.07	1.12	1.17	1.22	1.28	1.33	1.38	1.43	1.48	1.53	1.58									
42	1.09	1.14	1.20	1.25	1.30	1.35	1.40	1.46	1.51	1.56										
43	1.11	1.17	1.22	1.27	1.33	1.38	1.43	1.48	1.54	1.59										
44	1.13	1.19	1.24	1.30	1.35	1.40	1.46	1.51	1.57											
45	1.16	1.21	1.27	1.32	1.38	1.43	1.49	1.54	1.60											
46	1.18	1.23	1.29	1.34	1.40	1.46	1.51	1.57												
47	1.20	1.25	1.31	1.37	1.43	1.48	1.54	1.60												
48	1.22	1.28	1.33	1.39	1.45	1.51	1.57													
49	1.24	1.30	1.36	1.42	1.48	1.53	1.59													
50	1.26	1.32	1.38	1.44	1.50	1.56														
51	1.28	1.34	1.40	1.46	1.53	1.59														
52	1.30	1.36	1.43	1.49	1.55															
53	1.32	1.39	1.45	1.51	1.58															
54	1.34	1.41	1.47	1.54	1.60															
55	1.37	1.43	1.50	1.56																
56	1.39	1.45	1.52	1.58																
57	1.41	1.47	1.54	1.61																
58	1.43	1.50	1.56																	
59	1.45	1.52	1.59																	
60	1.47	1.54	1.61																	
61	1.49	1.56																		
62	1.51	1.58																		
63	1.53	1.61																		
64	1.55																			
65	1.58																			
66	1.60																			

O2 in Mix

	50%	60%	70%	80%	90%	100%
1	0.55	0.66	0.77	0.88	0.99	1.10
2	0.60	0.72	0.84	0.96	1.08	1.20
3	0.65	0.78	0.91	1.04	1.17	1.30
4	0.70	0.84	0.98	1.12	1.26	1.40
5	0.75	0.90	1.05	1.20	1.35	1.50
6	0.80	0.96	1.12	1.28	1.44	1.60
7	0.85	1.02	1.19	1.36	1.53	
8	0.90	1.08	1.26	1.44		
9	0.95	1.14	1.33	1.52		
10	1.00	1.20	1.40	1.60		
11	1.05	1.26	1.47			
12	1.10	1.32	1.54			
13	1.15	1.38	1.61			
14	1.20	1.44				
15	1.25	1.50				
16	1.30	1.56				
17	1.35					
18	1.40					
19	1.45					
20	1.50					
21	1.55					
22	1.60					

Equivalent Air Depth Table - Metric

		FRACTION OF OXYGEN (FO2) AND ACTUAL DEPTHS (METERS OF SEAWATER)															
		0.25	0.26	0.27	0.28	0.29	0.30	0.31	0.32	0.33	0.34	0.35	0.36	0.37	0.38	0.39	0.40
T O A I R T A B L E	9	8	8	8	8	7	7	7	6	6	6	6	6	5	5	5	4
	12	11	11	10	10	10	9	9	9	9	8	8	8	8	7	7	7
	15	14	13	13	13	12	12	12	12	11	11	11	10	10	10	9	9
	18	17	16	16	16	15	15	14	14	14	13	15	13	12	12	12	11
	21	19	19	19	18	18	17	17	17	16	16	16	15	15	14	14	14
	24	22	22	21	21	20	20	19	19	18	18	18	18	17	17	16	16
	27	25	25	24	24	23	23	22	22	21	21	20	20	20	19	19	19
	30	28	27	27	26	26	25	25	24	24	23	23	22	22	21	21	20
	33	31	30	30	29	29	28	28	27	26	26	25	25	24			
	36	34	33	33	32	31	31	30	30	29	28						
	39	37	36	35	35	34	33	33	32								
	42	39	39	38	37	37	36										
	45	42	42	41	40	39											
	48	45	44	44													
	51	48	47														
	54	51															

PO₂ Table - Metric

O₂ Time Limit	PO₂	Fraction of Oxygen (FO₂) and Actual Depths (Meters of Seawater)															
300	1.0	30	29	27	26	24	23	22	21	20	19	18	17	17	16	15	15
240	1.1	34	32	31	29	28	27	25	24	23	22	21	21	20	19	18	17
210	1.2	38	36	34	33	31	30	29	27	26	25	24	23	22	21	21	20
180	1.3	42	40	38	36	35	33	32	31	29	28	27	26	25	24	23	22
150	1.4	46	44	42	40	38	37	35	34	32	31	30	29	28	26	26	25
120	1.5	50	47	45	44	42	40	38	37	35	34	33	32	30	29	28	27
45	1.6	54	51	49	47	45	43	41	40	39	37	36	34	33	32	31	30

About TDI/SDI

About TDI

TDI was formed in 1994 by some of diving's most experienced instructors to bring technical applications of the sport to a wider audience. TDI's library of training materials and texts have become known as the industry's best and most professional resources. Most importantly, TDI has the best safety record of all training agencies.

Whether your interests lie in nitrox, rebreathers, mixed gas or any of the many other programs that TDI offers you can be assured that you will be participating in training that offers you the "cutting edge" of diving technology. With offices worldwide and over 10,000 instructors teaching our programs, TDI has become the largest international specialized dive agency.

About SDI

SDI grew out of the success of our sister company TDI, which specialized in more advanced disciplines of dive training. Our instructors asked for an entry level scuba training program that would reflect that same forward-looking approach that TDI brought to technical diving pursuits.

Finally after a year in development, the SDI training program was launched at the 1999 DEMA show. It was an instant success on its own merits. Both students and instructors have embraced the no nonsense approach that the SDI training system offers. We have streamlined the course materials to let students study the essential academics with a renewed emphasis on practical diving skills learned in both the pool and open water environments. And SDI was the first to require students to be taught with modern dive computers from the outset.

Diving is constantly changing. Many other agencies are still mired in yesterday while our staff looks ahead to the millennium and strives to continue our record as the innovators of the industry. We want to make the experience of diving one that is enjoyed by every family member to the fullest. As SDI we are all divers and want to share our love of the sport with as wide an audience as possible. Please check out the variety of programs at SDI and join us in our passion!

SDI DIVER PROGRAMS

SCUBA DIVING INTERNATIONAL

Open Water Diver
▼
Advanced Diver Development Program
◄ **(4 Specialty Diver Courses)**
▼
Advanced Diver ► **Solo Diver**
▼
Rescue Diver ► **Divemaster**
▼   ▼
Master Diver Program   **Assistant Instructor**
◄ **(8 Specialty Diver Courses)**   ▼
                            Instructor ◄
                            ▼
                    Instructor Trainer

- Altitude Diver
- Boat Diver
- Computer Diver
- Computer Nitrox Diver
- CPROX Administrator
- CPR1st Administrator
- Deep Diver(130ft Max)
- Diver Propulsion Vehicle
- Drift Diver
- Dry Suit Diver
- Equipment Specialist
- Ice Diver
- Marine Ecosystems Awareness
- Night/ Limited Visibility Diver
- Research Diver
- Search & Recovery Diver
- Shore/Beach Diver
- Underwater Navigation
- Underwater Photography
- Underwater Video
- Wreck Diver
- Underwater Hunter & Collector

Glossary

blender: a person who has been specially trained to fill nitrox cylinders.

CNS oxygen limit: the maximum exposure a diver can have to elevated levels of oxygen at depth, expressed as a percentage with the maximum exposure equal to 100%. This terminology is used by many nitrox dive computers and is part of the information displayed to the diver while using these computers. May also be expressed by other terms, according to the manufacturer.

commercial diver: a diver who works underwater for money, usually performing heavy construction work.

CONventid: an acronym for the signs and symptoms of oxygen poisoning. CON stands for convulsions. V= visual disturbances or hallucinations, E= ears or auditory hallucinations, N= nausea, t=twitching of muscles, I= irritability or apprehension, D=dizziness.

DCS: an abbreviation of decompression sickness.

decompression sickness: symptoms produced in a diver by nitrogen bubbles that have formed following an ascent, as a result of the absorption of excess nitrogen gas at depth. Depending on where the nitrogen bubbles lodge, they can cause the diver pain, paralysis, loss of coordination, loss of bladder or bowel control, and other symptoms.

decompression stop: a stop in the water at the end of a dive to allow the excess nitrogen that was absorbed at depth to exit the diver's body through his lungs, thus helping to avoid decompression sickness. Decompression stops can be calculated by using special dive tables or by using a dive computer. Stops are for specified times and depths.

EAN: an abbreviation that stands for enriched air nitrox.

EANx: an abbreviation that stands for enriched air nitrox when the oxygen percentage is not stated.

enriched air: another way that people refer to enriched air nitrox.

equivalent air depth: a calculation that shows that the pressure of nitrogen and oxygen in a nitrox mixture at a given depth is the same as breathing air at a shallower depth.

FO2: an abbreviation that stands for the term "fraction of oxygen." This is the decimal equivalent of the percentage of oxygen in the mixture.

fraction of oxygen: see FO$_2$.

fuel cell: a metal cylinder, similar in appearance to a battery, that is filled with chemicals that react with the oxygen in a gas mixture. When a fuel cell is installed in an oxygen analyzer, and the gas mixture in question is flowed past the fuel cell, this device will give a reading of the exact percentage of oxygen in the mix.

fully-closed circuit rebreather: a type of scuba unit that recirculates the diver's breathing gas and emits no bubbles. Oxygen is replaced as it is consumed and carbon dioxide is removed by chemical absorbents. Other gases used in this type of rebreather may include helium and/or nitrogen.

maximum operating depth: the maximum depth to which a particular nitrox breathing mixture may be used.

M.O.D.: an abbreviation for maximum operating depth.

nitrox: any gas mixture that contains nitrogen and oxygen, but usually refers to mixtures containing more than 21% oxygen.

nitrox blender: a person who has been specially trained to fill nitrox diving cylinders.

nitrox filling station: a dive store that has the capability to fill nitrox cylinders. May also be used to refer to the machinery used to fill nitrox cylinders.

nitrox tag: a plastic tag that can be written on and is designed to hang from a scuba cylinder valve to identify the nitrogen mixture inside the tank.

NOAA Nitrox I or II: nitrox mixtures commonly used by the National Oceanic and Atmospheric Administration. Nitrox I contains 32% oxygen and Nitrox II contains 36% oxygen.

OTL: an abbreviation for Oxygen Time Limit.

Glossary

OTU: an abbreviation that stands for Oxygen Tolerance Units.

oxygen analyzer: an electronic device used to measure the percentage of oxygen in a gas mixture.

oxygen clean: equipment that has been specially cleaned for oxygen service and contains oxygen compatible lubricants, seats, and o-ring seals.

oxygen compatible: lubricants and materials designed to be used with gas mixtures that contain 41% or more oxygen.

oxygen enriched air: any gas mixture containing more than 21% oxygen, and some amount of nitrogen.

oxygen limit fraction: a measurement made by a dive computer of a diver's exposure to elevated levels of oxygen, expressed in terms of a percentage. The maximum oxygen limit fraction would be 100%, which is to be avoided. Exposure to mixtures rich in oxygen for extended periods underwater can lead to oxygen poisoning.

oxygen poisoning: a physiological reaction that occurs in a diver's body after breathing mixtures containing oxygen at depth. The higher the percentage of oxygen in the mixture, the shallower the depth at which oxygen poisoning may occur. Oxygen poisoning may end in a convulsion. Oxygen poisoning is the same as oxygen toxicity.

oxygen safe lubricant: lubricants that are deemed compatible with breathing gas mixtures containing 41% or more oxygen.

oxygen service: equipment that has been specially cleaned for use with enriched air mixtures, and uses materials compatible with oxygen, such as regulator seats, o-rings, and other components.

oxygen time limit: the maximum amount of time a diver may be exposed to a given mixture containing nitrox with an acceptably low risk of experiencing oxygen toxicity.

oxygen tolerance unit: this is a term used to define a measurement of a diver's exposure to enriched air mixtures. This term is rarely used today.

oxygen toxicity: see oxygen poisoning

partial pressure: the pressure exerted by a gas in a mixture of gases.

PO_2: the partial pressure of oxygen in a mixture of gases.

precautionary decompression stop: see safety stop.

recompression chamber: A large metal cylinder fitted with valves and gauges, designed to treat a diver suffering from decompression sickness, by pressurizing the chamber internally with the diver inside. Also known as a hyperbaric chamber or a decompression chamber.

recompression treatment: a specified procedure for pressurizing a diver in a recompression chamber and slowly decompressing the diver while he breathes pure oxygen.

SafeAir: another term used to describe nitrox.

safety stop: a stop made in the water by a diver at the end of a dive when no decompression is required to help avoid decompression sickness. Safety stops are normally made at depths of 10-15 feet for 3-5 minutes.

semi-closed circuit rebreather: a type of breathing apparatus that recirculates most of the breathing gas a diver uses with each breath. Oxygen is replaced and carbon dioxide is removed. This type of rebreather typically uses nitrox mixtures.

surface interval: time spent on the surface between dives.

tank wrap: identifying tape attached to the circumference of a scuba cylinder used to identify it as a cylinder that is filled with nitrox.

technical diver: divers who engage in diving beyond the sport diving range but for the purpose of recreation.

tri-mix: a gas mixture containing three gases, usually oxygen, nitrogen, and helium. Used for deep diving.

About the Author - Steven M. Barsky

© Bob Evans/La Mer Bleu Productions

Steve Barsky started diving in 1965 in Los Angeles County, and became a diving instructor in 1970. His first employment in the industry was with a dive store in Los Angeles and he went on to work for almost 10 years in the retail dive store environment.

Steve attended the University of California at Santa Barbara, where he earned a Masters Degree in 1976 in Human Factors/Ergonomics. This has helped greatly in his thorough understanding of diving equipment design and use. His master's thesis was one of the first to deal with the use of underwater video systems in commercial diving. His work was a pioneering effort at the time (1976) and was used by the Navy in developing applications for underwater video systems.

His background includes being a commercial diver, working in the off-shore oil industry in the North Sea, Gulf of Mexico, and South America. He worked as both an air diving supervisor and a mixed gas saturation diver, making working dives down to 580'.

Barsky was marketing manager for Viking America, Inc., an international manufacturer of dry suits. He also served in a similar position at Diving Systems International (DSI), the world's leading manufacturer of commercial diving helmets.

Steve is an accomplished underwater photographer. His photos have been used in numerous magazine articles, catalogs, advertising, training programs, and textbooks.

A prolific writer, Barsky's work has been published in *Sea Technology, Skin*

Diver, Offshore Magazine, Emergency, Fire Engineering, Dive Training Magazine, Searchlines, Sources, Undersea Biomedical Reports, Santa Barbara Magazine, Underwater Magazine, and many other publications. He is the author of the *Dry Suit Diving Manual, Diving in High Risk Environments, California Lobster Diving, Spearfishing for Skin and Scuba Divers, Small Boat Diving, Diving with the EXO-26 Full Face Mask, Diving with the Divator MK II Full Face Mask,* and a joint author with Dick Long and Bob Stinton of *Dry Suit Diving: A Guide to Diving Dry.* Steve has taught numerous workshops on contaminated water diving, dry suits, small boat diving, spearfishing, and other diving topics. *The Simple Guide to Rebreather Diving* was written by Steve along with Mark Thurlow and Mike Ward.

In 1989 Steve formed Marine Marketing and Consulting, based in Santa Barbara, California. The company provides market research, marketing plans, consulting, newsletters, promotional articles, technical manuals, and other services for the diving and ocean industry. He has consulted to Dräger, AquaLung/U.S. Divers Co., Inc, Zeagle Systems, Inc., Diving Unlimited Intnl., Diving Systems Intnl, DAN, NAUI, and numerous other companies.

He also investigates diving accidents and serves as an expert witness in dive accident litigation.

In 1999, Steve and his wife Kristine formed Hammerhead Press to publish high quality diving books. Hammerhead Press is a subsidiary of the Carcharodon Corporation.

Steve is an instructor with SDI, TDI, NAUI, and PADI. You can purchase Steve's other books at your local dive store, or on-line at http://www.hammerheadpress.com/

Index